Surviving as a Teenager in a Grown-up's World

Surviving as a Teenager in a Grown-up's World

SHANE R. BARKER

BOOKCRAFT
SALT LAKE CITY, UTAH

For Shawna and Dallon

Library of Congress Catalog Card Number: 93-70992
ISBN 0-88494-881-1

First Printing, 1993

Printed in the United States of America

CONTENTS

1	The Law of Quit, Keep, and Start	1
2	In One Ear and Out the Other	9
3	C's and D's on the Report Card	21
4	Trying to Buy a Motorcycle	31
5	What If the Osmond Brothers All Sang Bass?	41
6	There's a Cowgirl in the Hallway!	51
7	I've Been Grounded Until I'm Twenty-One	61
8	A Friend Named Edweird	69
9	Chipmunks, Sunflower Seeds, and the Cosby Show	79
10	That's No Creature, That's My Teacher!	89
11	The Battle of Maple Dell	101
12	They Didn't Have Dentists in the Book of Mormon!	113
13	Ranting, Raving, and Blowing Your Cool	123
14	Climbing in the Rocks	131

1

THE LAW OF QUIT, KEEP, AND START

Surviving as a Teenager in a Grown-up's World

Coach Becker slammed his clipboard to the floor. His teeth were clenched and his face was knotted up like a fist. His eyes blazed with anger.

"No, no, *no!*" he shouted, storming onto the basketball court. "You can *not* just stand there and expect this play to happen! You have to *pop* the ball to the wing and *immediately* cut through the lane. You have to move fast. Understand that? *Fast!* Now come on . . . quit playing like a bunch of girls and do it right!"

Jeff Whiting sighed as he dribbled the ball back to midcourt and prepared to run the play again. Fourteen years old, he played point guard on his school's freshman basketball team. Quick with his hands and fast on his feet, Jeff had a knack for seeing the court and finding the open man. He could outdribble everyone else on the team. And he was deadly from three-point range.

But Jeff wasn't happy. Like everyone else on the team, he hated his coach.

"He yells at us for everything," Jeff said. "If we miss a shot he yells at us for not passing. If we dish off he yells at us for not shooting. It's like we can't do anything right."

And that wasn't the only problem. The coach was so strict that if a single player was late to practice, the whole team had to run laps. If anyone goofed off, the team ran more laps. The coach had his players so demoralized that they put about as much enthusiasm into basketball as they might put into scrubbing a bathroom floor.

But the worst thing was that there just wasn't any communication between the coach and his team. One day I heard Jeff and a player named Steve discussing what was happening.

"Why don't you talk to your coach about it?" I asked. "Tell him how you feel?"

Jeff looked shocked. "Are you kidding! If we ever said anything like that he'd scream and yell and make us run laps."

"Yeah," Steve agreed. "And *then* he'd get mad."

Jeff's team didn't do very well that season. And many of the players didn't even try out the next year. All because they had a tough time dealing with their coach.

Have you ever had an experience like that?

I have! After all, it's a grown-up's world. And to get along in it, you've got to play by their rules.

Sound tough?

It's not really. In fact, if you go about it right, you can do more than just survive in this world. You can excel, succeed, and have a whole lot of fun, too.

Let's look at a couple of ways to get started.

First, remember that it's your world too. And even though you're young, you *can* make a difference in it.

I know a young woman named Jennie who's the student representative of her school's Parent-Teacher-Student Association. She's normally cheerful and energetic, but when I saw her at Back-to-School Night she was looking a little miffed.

"What's wrong?" I asked.

"It's Mrs. Henry, the PTSA president," she said. "We're trying to choose a PTSA board, and she wants to let everyone and their little sister join."

I had no idea what she was talking about, so she explained.

"We're trying to get the students more involved," she said. "So one of the things we're doing is creating a student board. Mrs. Henry thinks we ought to accept every person who submits an application."

"So?"

"So the problem is that half the school wants to join. With that many people, we'll never be able to get anything done."

Jennie told me that she had tried to explain all this to Mrs. Henry, but that the PTSA president wouldn't listen.

As I talked with her, I realized that Jennie actually had *two* concerns. She was worried about the number of students applying for positions on the board. But she was also bothered that Mrs. Henry wasn't taking Jennie's concerns seriously.

The difficulties didn't get resolved, in fact, until Mrs. Henry actually saw the number of applications. Then, for the first time she realized that Jennie was right. There *were* too many people.

At that point things could have gotten messy, but Jennie was ready. "I knew what was going to happen," she said, "so I made plans. I took all of the names and divided them up. Then I assigned them to committees. We kept our board to the right size and still let everyone participate who wanted to."

That was good thinking. And it's a good example of how a young person *can* succeed in a grown-up's world.

Remember that being young is a blessing. Your natural energy and zest for life can bring out the best in people of all ages.

So let it!

Start every day knowing that you belong in this world. Believe that there's a place for you. Attack life with all the confidence and energy you have.

Second, never be afraid to approach an adult with a suggestion.

You probably already know that the grown-ups in your life don't have all the answers. So if your parents are having a little trouble establishing rules for the family, offer up a few thoughts of your own. If your science class is unusually boring, don't simply complain to your friends about it; find a tactful way of showing your teacher a way to liven things up. If your team is 0–27, and you have an idea on how to improve this, tell the coach!

I know a young woman named Nicci whose family has a tradition called QKS.

"It stands for Quit, Keep, and Start," she explained. "Every so often my parents take one of us kids aside and say 'QKS.' Then they tell us one thing they want us to quit doing, one thing they want us to keep doing, and one thing they want us to start doing."

But it works both ways. The family also had a tradition of reading a page or two of something every night before dinner, and Nicci didn't like it. So during family home evening one week she surprised everyone by saying, "It's time for QKS."

As soon as she had everyone's attention she said: "I don't like reading together at the dinner table every night. It's okay if we read together *sometimes*. But it's hard to concentrate on what we're reading when there's a whole table full of food right in front of us. Besides, by the time we're done reading all the food's cold. I think we should quit."

Nicci then followed the rules by mentioning something she wanted the family to keep doing, and something she wanted them to start doing.

As it turned out, Nicci wasn't the only one who didn't like reading at the dinner table. And as a result of her suggestion, the family changed the tradition, deciding to read together earlier in the day.

The fact that you're young doesn't mean that you don't have any good ideas. As a teenager, in fact, you have insights and perspectives that might never occur to an older person. So don't be afraid to share them.

I used to coach a little league baseball team. I wasn't the best coach in the city, nor the most experienced, but I was anxious to learn. And I was always looking for new ideas. One day after practice my fifteen-year-old second baseman came up to talk.

"You always bring in Marc or Jon to substitute at shortstop," he told me. "But they're not all that strong. They have a hard time making the throw to first."

I nodded. Marc and Jon were good fielders, but they did have trouble making that throw.

"So what should we do?"

"Well, I can make the throw. So when you have to make a substitution, let one of *them* play second, and move *me* over to short."

I nodded again. It was the perfect solution. It was

so obvious, in fact, that I was embarrassed that I hadn't thought of it myself. As much as I wanted to be an all-knowing coach, I learned that my players had lots of good ideas, too. They deserved to be listened to.

And so do you.

Keep in mind that not every adult will be open to every idea you have. But don't let that keep you quiet. If you have an idea or a suggestion, don't be afraid to make it.

Finally, let the adults in your life know when they're on the right track.

It's sometimes hard dealing with adults. But it's often just as tough for grown-ups to deal with teenagers. After all, things aren't the same as when they were young. So let them know when they're making progress.

I happen to be a junior high school math teacher, and there's nothing that motivates me more than knowing that somebody likes my class. Once in a while a parent will tell me that his daughter enjoys my class, or that her son thinks I'm "rad."

Talk about pressure! I try to be a good teacher anyway; but once I learn that I'm getting through to someone, I feel I can't let them down. Whatever it is that I think I'm doing right, I go out of my way to keep it up.

Most people are like that.

So if your parents come up with a fun incentive program for getting everyone to do their chores, tell them how much you like it. If your boss lets you close the store by yourself one night, tell her how much you appreciate it. If your teacher presents an especially interesting lesson, let her know how much you learned.

This can be hard to do. But if adults know they're reaching you, they're likely to keep it up. So don't be afraid to go up to your coach and say something like:

"I really like the way you ran practice today. I feel I learned a lot."

It really is a grown-up's world. But it belongs to you, too. So use the excellence and quality of *your* life to motivate and influence the adults you deal with. Offer suggestions when you have them. And let them know when they're doing right.

As you do these things you'll do more than just survive in this world. You'll have more fun and success than you ever thought was possible.

Tips to Remember

- Be glad you're young! Attack life with the energy of a whirlwind. Use your youthful energy and enthusiasm to motivate and influence people of all ages.

- Remember that it's your world, too. So don't wait to contribute until you grow up. Go out now and do your best in everything you do.

- Never be afraid to approach an adult with a suggestion. You have thoughts, insights, and ideas that might never occur to an older person. Share them.

- Let the adults in your life know when they're doing things you like. When they realize that they're reaching you, they're more likely to keep it up.

2

IN ONE EAR AND
OUT THE OTHER

Getting Adults to Listen

Jennifer Sharp's father, who had just come home from work, was relaxing in his favorite easy chair, settling down with the evening paper before dinner. He turned to the sports section as Jennifer read to him a couple of phone messages she'd taken before he came home.

"Uncle David called to see if you're going fishing with him Saturday," she said.

Her father nodded. "Uh, huh," he said from behind the paper.

"And Mr. Hodges called from the agency. He said not to worry about the meeting tomorrow morning. Somebody got sick, so they're going to postpone it until Friday."

Mr. Sharp nodded again as he searched the paper for a story on the previous night's Celtics game.

"And would it be okay if I went to the mall with Holly tonight?"

"Sure, Jen."

"Would you pick us up at eight?"

"Sure, Jen."

"Great! We'll be waiting at the south doors."

Jennifer and Holly spent the next couple of hours wandering through the mall. At eight o'clock, though, Mr. Sharp wasn't there to pick them up. The two girls waited until eight-thirty, then Jennifer phoned home.

"Dad, we've been waiting for half an hour," she said. "Where are you?"

Mr. Sharp sounded embarrassed. "Was I supposed to pick you up?"

"Yes! At eight o'clock!"

Jennifer eventually got her ride home, but she was still pretty annoyed with her father. He'd completely forgotten to pick her up, mostly because he hadn't been listening to her in the first place.

Have you ever spent time talking with an adult, only to feel as if everything you said went in one ear and out the other? Or have you ever needed to talk with a parent, teacher, or employer, only to feel she or he wasn't interested in what you had to say?

I have. When I was in junior high school, one day I was watching my math teacher work out a complicated problem on the chalkboard when I noticed that he'd made a mistake. I quickly raised my hand.

"Mr. Blacker!"

Mr. Blacker ignored me and kept right on working. I began waving my hand.

"Mr. Blacker!"

This time Mr. Blacker paused just long enough to say, "Shane, would you mind waiting until I'm finished?"

"But . . ."

Before I could say another word, he turned and wrote my name on the chalkboard as a warning not to say any more. I couldn't believe it!

"But Mr. Blacker . . ."

Mr. Blacker placed a check mark next to my name. That meant that I was getting deeper in trouble, and that I'd have to stay a few seconds after class. It also meant that I'd better shut up.

So I did. I folded my arms and sat back in my chair as Mr. Blacker continued work on the problem. After another few moments, though, he took a step back from the chalkboard and frowned.

"Humm," he said. "Something's not quite right here. Anyone see anything wrong?"

A girl in the front row raised her hand. "Up at the top you added 10 to the left side and you should have subtracted."

Mr. Blacker grinned sheepishly. "Ah, that's it. Thank you, Marilyn." He corrected his mistake, then turned to look at the class. "I made a pretty simple mistake," he said. "But I'm surprised that none of you caught it earlier."

At the time I felt hurt, because I *had* noticed it. And when I had raised my hand, I hadn't been trying to cause trouble. I was just trying to point out the mistake. I felt hurt because he hadn't been willing to listen to me.

I know a young woman named Tarryn Fisher who had a similar experience with her mother. Tarryn had just come home from school, and her mother was busy making a new dress on the sewing machine.

"Mom, Linda Haskell's having a pizza party tonight. Can I go?"

Mrs. Fisher adjusted a swatch of cloth, pulled a pin from the hem, then carefully ran a couple of inches of fabric through the machine. "That's fine, dear."

A few hours later, though, Tarryn was just getting ready to leave when her mother called her for dinner.

"I'm not eating tonight," Tarryn said. "I'm going to Linda's, remember?"

Mrs. Fisher shook her head. "It's Monday night, Tarryn, and we have a rule about staying home."

"But Mom, you told me I could!"

Just like Mr. Sharp, Mrs. Fisher hadn't been listening to her daughter, and the resulting mix-up hurt Tarryn's feelings. It was an innocent mistake, but it's one that happens all the time.

Just because most people have two ears, we believe that they're listening every time we talk to them. But in today's world most people have so much going on that it's often hard to get them to pay attention to one more thing. Sometimes they get busy, and sometimes they have other things on their minds. Most adults, in fact, have so much to think about that it's a wonder they hear anything we say at all.

When I was in the eighth grade, I once went to the dentist and in doing so missed an important history test. My teacher, Mr. Winger, had a strict policy concerning makeups, and I knew that I had just one week to take the test, either before or after school.

Now, that shouldn't have been a problem. But that particular week I happened to have basketball practice every day after school (believe me, we needed it) and the stage band I played in was rehearsing every morning (we were preparing for a region festival). So I asked Mr. Winger for permission to take the test a couple of days late. He nodded and said sure.

But the next Monday, when I went in to take the test, he shook his head.

"You have one week to make up missed work," he told me. "And you missed the deadline."

"But you told me I could take it late!"

Mr. Winger looked doubtful. "When did I tell you that?"

"Last Monday!"

Mr. Winger still looked unconvinced, and I realized that he probably hadn't been listening when I'd first talked with him. He didn't even remember talking to me! And I had to plead until I was blue in the face before he agreed to let me take the test.

Being able to talk with adults is an important survival skill. And once you learn how to do it, you'll be well on your way to getting along with them. But you can't talk with adults when they're not listening. So let's look at a couple of ways to get their attention.

First, *get them alone.*

If you really need someone's attention, you've got to have that person all to yourself. Having other people around will just give them more things to think about, and that's something you don't want.

A man I know, Mr. James, teaches German at a junior high school. He's a popular teacher, and many of his students like to visit with him in the mornings before school. I've often walked into his room and found a dozen or more students visiting and passing the time before their first class. The only trouble is that many of them want to talk with him—all at the same time. Typical "conversations" sound something like this:

Alice: Did you see the BYU game last night? We had seats on the fifth row where we could see everybody. Those guys are *soooo* cute!

Steve: Know what? My dad's taking us to Park City for Christmas. We're going to stay in a condominium that's only a block away from the ski lifts . . .

Kristy: Mrs. Hansen is making us read four hundred pages this month! Can you believe that? How are we ever supposed to read that much?

Jon: Mr. James, could you help me with this assignment? I don't understand what I'm supposed to be doing . . .

While all of this is going on, Mr. James usually just sits on the edge of his desk and smiles. And most of the time he's only half listening to the kids who are talking with him. This isn't because he's being rude. It's because there's just no way he can listen to everyone who's competing for his attention.

It's impossible for someone to concentrate on more than one thing at a time. And if an adult has to divide his attention between you and someone else, he's not going to be able to listen very well. If you really want someone to listen to you, then, get him alone. Find a place to talk where you won't be disturbed or interrupted.

Second, *find a place to talk where you won't be distracted.*

There's nothing like getting into a good discussion with someone, only to have the telephone ring or have a neighbor come barging in on you.

When I was in high school, I once went to talk with a man named Jack about a decision I had to make. I needed his help, and I needed to hear what advice he could give me. But we hadn't been talking for more than a minute when the telephone rang and he had to leave to answer it.

A few minutes after he returned, his two-year-old daughter waddled into the room. She wanted to crawl all over the furniture and play with delicate knick-knacks on the lamp stand. Jack had to keep such a close eye on her that he wasn't able to concentrate on me. Then, when his daughter left and I thought I finally had him to myself, the phone rang again.

If you really want someone's attention, you must get him away from distractions—away from telephones, secretaries, television sets, and so on. You have to get him in a place where he won't have anything to think about but you.

Third, *pick a good time to talk.*

If you try talking with your football coach just moments before a big game, he's probably going to have a hard time concentrating on what you have to say. He's probably wound up tighter than a clock anyway, and he's going to have a lot on his mind. He's not going to have the time or the patience for an intimate talk.

A young woman named Jeanie once needed to talk with her English teacher about a problem she was having in his class. But when she went in to see him he was gruff and abrupt and not very willing to talk. The problem was that Jeanie went to see him just ten minutes before his first-period class; and like many teachers, he was still preparing himself for a day of school and had a lot of things on his mind.

So Jeanie just waited until after school. Then, when most people had gone home and things were a little more quiet and relaxed, her teacher sat down and had a good talk with her.

Remember that if you need to talk with your mother and she has to present a homemaking lesson in an hour's time, it might be better to wait for another time. This doesn't mean that her lesson is more important than you are. But if she already has the lesson on her mind, it might be hard to channel her attention in another direction.

And when your father is getting ready for work, he's likely to have a lot on his mind, too. He needs to think about appointments he has that day and how he's going to handle them. He may have a big meeting he's nervous about.

Teachers are the same way. In the half hour or so before school they are often bombarded by students needing something or other, and many teachers may still be preparing for their lessons that day. They're gearing up for a day of work, and they're often a little uptight. So that's *not* usually the best time to talk with them.

If you really need to talk with your parents, the best time is usually sometime after they get home from work. Give them a little while to relax and unwind, and then get them away for a talk.

If you need to talk with a teacher, the best time is usually after school. The day is almost over for teachers then, and they're generally more relaxed and friendly than they are in the morning. (If your teacher has a free class period—as many of them do—you might also see if you can be excused from another class to see him.)

If you want to talk with your employer about a raise, a problem, time off, or anything else that's important, it's best to make an appointment with her. Be professional. Don't just approach her out of the blue when she may be busy or thinking about other things.

Fourth, *tell him that you have something serious to say.*

Let your teachers, parents, or employer know that their attention is important to you.

A young woman I know named Rachelle clowns around a lot. She's always smiling and laughing and telling jokes, and she loves to tease people. But one day she came to me with a problem.

"I'm failing my geography class," she told me.

"You're failing every class," I teased her, not realizing that she was being serious for a change.

Rachelle smiled, then continued. "Miss Correy told

me that I'm missing a whole bunch of book reports, and she can't find my research paper, either."

"I'm not surprised," I said. "You're about as organized as a black hole."

Rachelle's eyes welled up with tears. "I'm serious. My parents'll kill me if I fail a class."

Until that moment, I hadn't realized that Rachelle really was trying to be serious. Generally she joked about her classes so much that until then I just thought she was goofing around again.

It may be the same with you. Sometime you might have something to discuss with an adult who doesn't understand how serious your problem is. Don't take any chances. Tell him up front that what you're talking about is important. Let him know that you mean business.

I once spent a summer working as the program director of a Boy Scout aquatics base, and I often had young Scouts come to talk with me. One time I was sitting in my office when a twelve-year-old Scout named Chris knocked on the door.

"C'mon in," I said, pulling up a chair. "Have a seat."

Chris shut the door behind him and sat down. "I really need to talk to you about something that happened yesterday," he said. "I'm really worried about it."

I put my work down and listened as he talked. It turned out that solving Chris's problem wasn't really very difficult. But the point is that once he told me he had a problem and he needed my help, I was all ears. I was honored that he was confiding in me, and I was anxious to do all I could to help.

You will often have to do the same thing.

Finally, *don't ever be afraid to talk with an adult.*

After all, adults have been in many of the same

jams you'll get into, so they might have a few suggestions for getting out. Besides that, most people will
consider it a compliment to have you confide in them.
It shows that you trust their judgment and value their
opinion. It may help to bring you closer together.

If all adults would just listen when you needed to
talk, most of the problems you have with them would
disappear. But adults aren't much different from you,
and they don't always pay attention. Sometimes
they're busy, and sometimes they just have other
things on their mind.

If you really need to have someone listen to you,
then, remember to get the person alone. Find a place
to talk where you won't be interrupted or distracted.
Choose a time when you know the person won't have
other things to think about. Make clear that you have
something serious to say, and that it's important that
he listen to you.

As you do this, you'll be better able to get through
to the adults you deal with. And you'll be well on your
way to surviving in their world.

Tips to Remember

- If you *really* need someone's complete attention,
  get him alone. Don't share him with anyone. Remember that if anyone else is around, your adult
  is not going to be able to concentrate on *you*.

- Find a place to talk where you won't be distracted. Go to a park, or the library, or just sit

out in the car. Take care to avoid places with secretaries, clocks, and (especially) telephones.

- Wait for a good time to talk. Choose a time when the person is not in a hurry to go somewhere or get something done. And remember that most adults are easiest to talk with *after* work than before.

- Tell him up front that you need his attention; that this is going to be a serious talk and that it's important to you. Get his attention before you start talking.

- If you make an agreement with an adult, don't be afraid to remind him about it. If you're expecting a teacher to help you after school, for instance, don't be afraid to say, "Is it still okay for me to come in tomorrow after school?" And if you make an agreement with your parents, don't hesitate to leave simple reminders taped to the refrigerator.

- Don't ever be afraid to talk with an adult. Most of them will appreciate your confidence and will draw closer to you because of it.

3

C'S AND D'S ON
THE REPORT CARD

Getting Adults to See the Best in You

The bat cracked as the ball shot toward the outfield fence, and Chris Gates dashed for first base. He hit the bag at top speed and turned toward second.

The center fielder charged after the ball, scooping it out of the grass and rifling it toward second. Chris slid face-first in the dirt, beating the ball by a whisker.

"All right, Chris!" someone shouted. "Way to hit the ball! Good job out there!"

Chris stood up and dusted red dirt from his uniform. He grinned.

Chris played third base on his high school's sophomore baseball team. He was a powerful hitter and was one of the best fielders on the team.

One time, during a game against a rival school, Chris was standing just inside the third-base line when the batter cracked a shot straight toward left field. Chris leaped for the ball like an F-16 going for takeoff. He went straight up, putting his glove into space just as the ball got there. He curled up and hit the ground rolling, but still managed to hang on to the ball.

Another time, a batter sliced a grounder that went smoking through the grass toward third base. As quick as a cat, Chris darted after it. He knew the ball was going to be just out of reach, so he dived for it. But while he was in the air the ball hit something and bounced to the side. Chris had to reach behind him, catching the ball with his bare hand before he smacked into the grass.

It was the most spectacular play I'd ever seen. Or at least it would have been, except for one thing: Chris tried to throw the ball.

Jumping to his feet, he took quick aim and rifled the ball toward first. He overshot the first baseman by about three feet, not only allowing the runner to make base, but letting him reach second, too.

The coach came screaming from the dugout.

"What in the world are you trying to do?" he shouted. "That guy's not seven feet tall! You've got to keep the ball down so that he can at least have a shot at *jumping* for it!"

Now, Chris felt bad enough about his mistake. Making a bad throw had allowed a man on base. And it nearly cost his team the game.

"Fielding's never been a problem for me," he told me. "I'm quick on my feet and I hardly even have to look at the ball. I know where it's going and I just seem to get my glove in the right place at the right time. But throwing . . ." He shook his head. "Well, I'm not really very accurate."

It wasn't that he didn't try. He used to practice all the time. Standing out on the grass behind the school he would practice throwing for hours. But it didn't help. No matter how much he practiced, he couldn't throw the ball in a straight line.

"Everybody tells me I throw like a girl," he said. "But I've never been able to change that. There's something about my arm . . . it just won't rotate the way it's supposed to."

The sad thing is that it was always getting him in trouble with his coaches.

Finally, tired of getting yelled at all the time, Chris tried something different. He went to the coach and asked to play somewhere besides third base.

"I told him that I was the best fielder on the team," he said. "And I told him that I was a good hitter, too. All we needed was to find a place where my throwing wouldn't hurt us so much."

Chris was convincing enough that the coach was willing to give him a chance. So Chris moved from third base to first. There, his spectacular fielding was an asset. And though he occasionally muffed a double play on the throw to second, his poor throwing wasn't a major liability.

Chris was the team MVP that season, and the next year he made the high school varsity team. All because he was able to get his coach to look past his weak point and see his best.

Have you ever noticed how often adults look past *your* good points? It doesn't matter how many A's you have on your report card; all they ever seem to notice are the C's and D's. No matter how well you clean up the yard, they still complain about the mess in your bedroom. No matter how many points you score in the game, they're still uptight because you missed those foul shots.

Isn't that true?

Most adults don't do this on purpose. But reacting

quickly to the negative side of things almost seems to be human nature. You probably even do it yourself.

I have a friend named Terrence who once spent a whole afternoon working in the backyard so his father wouldn't have to. But as soon as his father got home, Terrence got yelled at for tracking grass through the house. No one even noticed all the work he'd done in the yard.

A young woman named Susan told me a similar story. After washing her school clothes one Saturday, she did the rest of the family's laundry as well. She wasn't even finished before she was in trouble for not having the family room dusted.

"It's one thing to get yelled at," she said. "But no one even thanked me for all the work I *did* do. No one noticed that I was just trying to help out."

I remember a time when a friend asked me to read an English paper for her. I took a note pad and jotted down all the mistakes I noticed as I read. I listed spelling errors, grammatical problems, and punctuation difficulties.

It wasn't long before I had quite a list. The funny thing was that it really was a good paper. All it needed was to be polished up a bit. But in trying to make the paper better, I wasn't looking for good things. I was deliberately looking for mistakes.

In trying to help you, many adults may do the same thing. They may only fill in your "need-to-fix" column and ignore the things that you're doing well. Sometimes they get so carried away that it's easy for them—and you—to forget that you even have any good points.

If that starts happening to you, you have to show them that you're trying.

I have a friend named Lisa who struggled in geometry. She tried hard and she studied a lot more than most kids, but she still had a rough time. No matter how much effort she put into her study, she still had trouble understanding what was going on.

One day Lisa decided to let her teacher know how hard she was trying. She spent a lot of time at home working problems over and over again, and every day when her teacher asked for the day's assignment, Lisa turned in all of her "extra" work too. She didn't get any points for it, but it showed her teacher how hard she was trying. It showed her teacher all of the extra time and work that her test scores didn't.

It worked, too. After all, there's nothing that impresses a teacher more than a student's going the extra mile in *his* class. And Lisa's teacher began spending more time with her. He realized that Lisa was struggling to learn, and *he* went the extra mile to help her understand.

So if the coach is mad because you can't dribble with your left hand, go early to practice and let him see you working on it. If your parents are unhappy because you haven't earned your Eagle, let them catch you working on merit badges. And if your band teacher is nagging you to learn the chromatic scale, spend a little time in the practice room to show him you're trying.

Most adults will be happy with you as long as they believe you're doing the best you can. Let them see you working on things. Let them know you're trying.

Next, learn to emphasize your strong points.

You need to remember that everyone has weaknesses. And everyone has strong points, too. Chris, the boy I introduced at the beginning of this chapter, had a terrible throwing arm. But he made up for that with his dazzling fielding and power at the plate.

Now, there are things that you don't do so well either. But you have talents and abilities that make up for that. The trick is to get people to focus on those things you do best.

I know a young woman named Kelly whose creative writing teacher was always nagging her about her handwriting. Every time Kelly turned in a story, Miss Parson made comments about her penmanship, but never about Kelly's style or creativity.

"I *knew* I had bad handwriting," Kelly said. "And I knew it was something I had to work on. But I really wanted to know what she thought about my stories."

So Kelly changed tactics. The next time she turned in a story, she *typed* it.

"It was a real pain," she said. "But for the first time Miss Parson focused on my story and not my handwriting."

When I was working at Boy Scout camp, a boy named Jason applied for a job. He had a resume as long as your arm, which was impressive for a boy just out of high school. He had experience at several different part-time jobs, and he had glowing recommendations. He had earned high grades and had been a member of the National Honor Society. He had also been a member of his student council.

Sound good? He sounded good to me!

The only trouble was that Jason was confined to a wheelchair.

In many places, his being in a wheelchair wouldn't have been a problem. But Boy Scout camp? Our camp featured lots of hills, trees, and rough, rugged terrain. Many older Scoutmasters (at least those who were out of shape) struggled to get from one end of camp to the other. One overweight man even collapsed on the trail once, scaring everyone into thinking he'd had a heart attack.

So it wasn't easy to picture a boy in a wheelchair having much fun there.

Jason just smiled as he talked with me about it. "It's always the same," he said. "People are always worried about the things I *can't* do. So I have to make them forget that I'm in a wheelchair. I have to get them thinking about all the things I *can* do."

Jason got his job at camp, mostly because he had a positive attitude and a sunny disposition that just didn't quit. But he didn't stop there. He went out of his way to participate in every event the camp offered. He shot at the rifle range. He canoed in the lake. He even joined in a relay race.

Finally, he attached a sign to his wheelchair that read, "Can Do."

"And it was great," he told me. "People were always asking me what it meant, and I told them it was to force them to think of all the things I *can* do."

Like Jason, you also have limitations. You may not have a knack for sports (which can be especially hard if you come from an athletic family). You may not be good at math. Or English. Or music.

But you're certain to have strengths in other areas. And you need to let people know what they are.

One way to do that is by sharing your successes. If you earn a bonus at work, for instance, tell your parents. If you score twenty points in a basketball game, tell your teachers about it. And if you get on the honor roll, tell your coaches.

This isn't bragging. It's a way of letting people see a side of you they might not know. It helps them to know you better.

Sharing your successes will also help your teachers, coaches, and employers get to know you as someone more than just another student or employee. They'll begin to see a new side to your personality.

They'll understand you better. And—believe it or not—they'll find it easier to tolerate your imperfections. They'll be more willing to look beyond your hang-ups.

I once had a boy in my eighth-grade algebra class who couldn't sit still for a minute at a time. He was constantly out of his seat, sharpening pencils, borrowing paper, or throwing things in the garbage.

He drove me crazy!

I had to admit that he was a good student. But the fact that he couldn't sit and be quiet drove me nuts.

Then, about the same time I was thinking I couldn't stand another minute of his behavior, he tried out for the school play. We were doing *The Sound of Music* that year, and Josh got the part of one of the Von Trapp boys.

"It's going to be *great*," he told me one day in class. "Are you going to come watch me?"

"I wouldn't miss it for the world," I told him.

And I didn't. But what surprised me was that he wasn't any different on stage than he was in class. It seemed more natural for him to be buzzing around on stage, but his actions weren't any different than normal. For the first time I began to realize that he wasn't trying to be a nuisance in class. That's just the way he was.

And even though his behavior in class didn't change, I found that I became more tolerant of him.

When the adults in your life begin to understand you, they too will start to overlook those little hang-ups that make us all human.

Finally, be tolerant of adults who are just trying to help.

A coach who constantly harps about your footwork isn't always trying to be a jerk. He just wants to help. A parent who insists that you earn good grades only wants you to realize your potential. A teacher who forces you to work just wants you to learn.

So even though it's annoying when an adult nags you to practice your trumpet, work on your dance steps, or read another chapter of some boring novel, don't get uptight. Recognize what they're trying to do. Accept the fact that they're only trying to help.

You can't be a teenager without having people on your case once in a while. But show them that you're trying. Get them to focus on those things you do well. Share your successes. Be tolerant of those adults who are just trying to help.

Most adults will respond. When they do, surviving in their world won't only be easier; it'll be a lot more fun, too!

Tips to Remember

- When people get after you for something you're having a hard time with, show them that you're trying. Let them catch you working on it. People are less likely to complain about your mistakes when they know that you're doing the best you can.

- Emphasize your strong points. Find ways to get people to focus on those things you do right.

- Share your successes. Remember that when people realize you're making progress in one area, they're more likely to accept a mistake or two somewhere else. (But keep in mind that being a great athlete doesn't mean that you're allowed to flunk English!)

- Be tolerant. This sometimes takes a lot of patience. But keep telling yourself that when people nag, they're usually just trying to help.

4

TRYING TO BUY
A MOTORCYCLE

Getting Adults to Trust You

Robbie Clarke waited until after class, then went up to talk with his eighth-grade science teacher.

"I'm not going to be here tomorrow," he said. "Could you tell me what our assignment's going to be so I can work on it over the weekend?"

Mr. Matthews took a moment to write a score on a student's homework journal before looking up. "We're not going to have an assignment," he said. "We're taking a test on chapter five, remember?"

Robbie rolled his eyes. "Oh, yeah. I forgot. Will I be able to make it up?"

Mr. Matthews nodded. "Certainly. You can come in anytime before or after school."

"Do I have to do it next week?"

"If you can. Is there a problem with that?"

"Not really. I just have a long way to walk home when I stay after."

Mr. Matthews took a moment to scan another journal, then reached into his desk and pulled out a copy of the test. "If I let you take this home, could I count on you to do your own work?"

Robbie's eyes lit up. "Yes!"

"And you wouldn't show it to anyone?"

"No!"

Matthews handed him the test. "You're an honest young man," he said. "I don't think you'd cheat."

Robbie didn't cheat, either. Mr. Matthews was strict when it came to taking tests, and Robbie knew that it wasn't like him to let a student take a test home. He knew that his teacher trusted him, and Robbie wasn't going to disappoint him.

If you're like most young people, you want other people to trust you. You want your parents, teachers, and other leaders to believe in you. You want to be free to do your own thing without having them always looking over your shoulder.

And that's great. It's nice to be trusted. But you need to remember that trust doesn't come easily. It doesn't come automatically. And it doesn't come unearned.

My friend Laura works part-time at a candy store in the town mall. She was working by herself one night when a woman came in to buy a box of chocolates. Laura filled the woman's order, took her money, and gave her change. The woman left but returned a few minutes later asking for her wallet.

"I haven't seen it," Laura said.

"But I left it right here on the counter!"

Laura looked around, but there wasn't a wallet anywhere. And she couldn't remember having seen one. She shrugged. "I'm sorry, but I haven't seen it."

With that, the woman became angry. She accused

Laura of stealing it. She stormed away, telling Laura that she was going to call the police.

Laura called her boss, who said he would come right down. As soon as Mr. McCann arrived, he looked Laura straight in the eyes and asked, "Did you take the wallet?"

Laura shook her head. "No. I didn't."

Mr. McCann nodded. "All right," he said. "I believe you."

And he left it at that. From that moment on, even when a police officer showed up to investigate, Mr. McCann backed Laura up one hundred percent. And he never questioned her about it again.

Mr. McCann wasn't just being a nice guy. Laura had worked for him for several months. Even though she was only eighteen, she sometimes opened the store for him on weekends and she often closed it at night. She often took charge of the till, counting the money, filling out receipts, and making bank deposits.

Mr. McCann knew from experience that he could trust Laura. He knew from working with her that she didn't lie and she didn't steal, so even when a customer flatly accused Laura of stealing, Mr. McCann believed in her.

When I was in junior high school I had a friend named Tyler who wanted to try out for the basketball team. He was a good athlete, but he wasn't a very good student. His parents worried that if he suddenly had ball practice every day his grades would suffer even more than usual.

So Tyler went to work. He put extra work into his classes and brought his grades up. His teachers noticed the change and his parents did, too. When the time came for him to try out for the team, his parents were no longer worried. Tyler had proven that he *could* do well in school and play ball at the same time.

I've always liked Tyler's approach. He went out and earned his parents' confidence *before* he needed it. When the time came to get their permission, he no longer had anything to prove.

Most people do this backwards. I know a young woman named Karen, for instance, who wanted to attend a concert, but her parents wouldn't let her. The problem was that Karen had the habit of staying out late, and she had broken her curfew many times.

"Please, let me go," she pleaded. "I *promise* I'll be home on time!"

The trouble with Karen's approach is that she was asking to be trusted when she really wasn't very trustworthy. She wanted her parents to believe in her when she'd never given them any reason to believe they could. They couldn't count on her to be home on time. They couldn't count on her to stay close to her friends or to avoid strangers. Karen had broken the rules too many times for her parents to believe that she'd do what they asked.

Expecting trust before you've earned it is like asking to be paid before you mow the lawn. It just doesn't happen. Just as an employer expects you to finish the job before he pays you, people need you to prove yourself before they give you their trust.

That may not seem fair. But that's the way it is. Trust is precious, and it doesn't come easily. So if you want to be trusted, pay the price. Prove to the people around you that you're worthy of *being* trusted.

I live near a boy named Sam who was once accused of setting off the school fire alarm. The principal called him into his office and questioned him for nearly an hour. Even though Sam insisted that he was innocent, the principal didn't believe him.

It took one of Sam's friends, in fact, to finally convince the principal that it must have been someone else.

"We were out on the football field when it happened," Jon explained. "We weren't even near the building."

And so the principal let him go. Jon's story was the same as Sam's, but the principal only believed it when Jon told it.

Why?

Easy. Sam had a reputation for pulling pranks. He had been in the principal's office many times before. He had trashed people's lockers, skipped classes, and generally made a nuisance of himself. Pulling the fire alarm was just the sort of thing he might do.

Jon, on the other hand, was just the opposite. He was a fun-loving boy, but he was a good student who rarely got into trouble. He had a reputation for being honest. So when *he* said that Sam was innocent, the principal believed him.

Again, it may not seem fair. But that's the way life is. If you are known as a troublemaker, you'll often be blamed for things you have not done.

But if you have a reputation for telling the truth, people will believe what you tell them. If you are known for being dependable, adults will be more likely to let you do your own thing. They'll believe in you because they'll know from experience that they can trust you.

You'll get exactly the amount of trust that you're willing to earn.

Take a minute and think about the reputation *you* are developing. When you tell your parents you'll be home by ten, do you make it? Or do you come straggling in thirty minutes late? When you borrow the family car, do you return it with a tankful of gas? Or do you leave it filled with crumbs and garbage from your pizza party the night before? If you have to be to work at seven, are you there on time? Or do you come sneaking in ten minutes late?

Again, you'll be given exactly the amount of trust you're willing to earn. So if you want to be trusted, pay the price. Do what it takes to be trusted.

More to the point, if you want to stay out at night, prove to your parents that you'll be home when they ask you to be. If you want to spend more time with your friends, prove that you'll still get your chores and homework done. If you want to borrow the family car, prove that you can take care of it.

A friend of mine named Brandon owned an old, battered jeep. It was fun to drive around, but it wasn't great for trying to impress anyone. It was cold and noisy and it bounced around a lot. So when Brandon got a date to the junior prom, he knew he had to find something else to drive.

Now, Brandon's father happened to own a nice, new car that was perfect. The only problem was that Brandon was an inexperienced driver. And his father wasn't excited about letting him take his car.

"It's an expensive car," his dad told him. "I don't think you're ready for it."

But Brandon kept pestering him until his dad finally gave in. The night of the prom, Brandon drove as carefully as he could. But after the dance he walked into the parking lot and found that someone had backed into his dad's car. The driver's door was bashed in so deep that it wouldn't even open.

Brandon's father didn't get mad as everyone thought he would. But he did tell Brandon that he expected him to get the damage repaired. The next day Brandon was out getting bids on the repair work.

The interesting thing is that from then on, Brandon's father let him borrow the car whenever he needed it. Brandon hadn't proven that the car was perfectly safe with him. But he *did* prove that he would take care of any problems that came up.

You need to do the same. Prove that you can handle responsibility. Prove that you deserve to be trusted.

One of the worst things about trust is that while it's difficult to earn, it's easy to lose. You might work for months—or even years—earning a person's trust, only to lose it with a single mistake.

I know a young woman named Ana, for instance, whose mother allowed her to spend the night with a friend. "But I want you to stay at Christy's," her mother said. "I don't want you going anywhere without my knowing about it."

Ana agreed, but soon after she got to Christy's the two girls decided to go to the mall. You've probably already guessed what happened next, and you're right. Ana's mother was there.

"I felt so awful," Ana told me. "I was embarrassed that she caught me. But worse than that was knowing that she wouldn't trust me anymore. I promised myself right then that I would never lie to her again, and I haven't."

It may not seem right, and it may not seem fair, but once you've lost a person's trust it's hard to get it back. That's why if you want to be trusted you've got to earn it. It's essential that you prove that you deserve it.

There's one more thing that you need to remember. No matter how trustworthy you are, things aren't always going to work out the way you want them to. When I was in high school, for instance, I wanted to buy a motorcycle. All of my friends had bikes, and I wanted one, too.

Now, if anyone had ever earned the right to buy a motorcycle, it was me. I earned good grades in school to keep my insurance rates down. I drove carefully and had never received a ticket. I studied hard for the motorcycle test and passed it with flying colors.

But my parents still said no.

The problem, as my father explained it to me, was that motorcycles were dangerous. He was a captain on the police force, and the motorcycle accidents he had seen convinced him that he didn't want any of his kids riding them.

At the time I felt hurt. I didn't think my parents trusted me. But I later realized that they did trust me. It was the motorcycle they didn't trust. I could have been the best driver in the world and they still wouldn't have let me buy one.

My friend Marcie had a similar experience. A sophomore in high school, she wanted to attend a rock concert with her friends.

Now, Marcie's parents knew that she was dependable. They knew that they could trust her. But they still said no.

Marcie accused her parents of not trusting her. But that wasn't the case at all. They knew from experience that she would be careful. They knew that she would be home on time. But they worried about the sort of people who would be at the concert. And they simply didn't want her in that sort of environment.

There will be times when your parents will be the same way. When it happens, don't take it personally. And don't be angry. Try talking things over if you need to, but remember that being a parent sometimes means being overprotective. Don't believe that your parents are simply not willing to trust you.

There's nothing that will smooth your dealings with adults more than proving that they can trust you.

So do it!

If you want to spend more time out of the house, prove that you can play and *still* get your chores done. Show your parents that you will *always* be home when they want you to be. If you want your boss to give you more responsibility, show her that you're mature enough to handle it. Work hard to make her job easier. Go the extra mile. Do things to help out without being asked.

As you do, you'll find that most adults *will* trust you. And you'll be well on your way to surviving in their world.

Tips to Remember

- Think about the reputation you're developing. Are you known for keeping your word? Or for being dependable? If not, then start! Do what it takes to earn the trust you want.

- Go out and earn people's confidence *now!* Then, when you need someone's trust, you won't have anything left to prove.

- Once you've earned someone's trust, move heaven and earth to keep it. Make your promises as solemn as contracts. Be obedient. Be dependable. Never lie. Stick by your commitments.

- Remember that things won't always work out the way you want them to. When they don't, try not to take it personally. Don't confuse someone's concern for you with a lack of trust.

5

WHAT IF THE OSMOND BROTHERS ALL SANG BASS?

Dealing with Expectations

Dad, no!"

Karilyn Peterson's father was wearing his deadly father-knows-best expression. "Believe me, Kari. It'll work. Now, come on . . . just give it a try."

"Dad, no! I'm *not* going to do it!"

"You don't have any choice, Kari. Believe me, it's the only way."

Karilyn couldn't believe her father was serious. Fifteen years old, she played guard on her school's sophomore basketball team. A natural team leader, she could run an offense better than many players on the high school varsity team. Besides that, she was a gifted shooter . . . especially from the foul line.

Karilyn's only weakness, in fact, was that she couldn't help looking down at the ball as she dribbled.

Rather than keeping her head up looking for open players, she was always looking down to see what her hands were doing.

But her father had a solution. He wanted to tie Karilyn's ponytail to her jersey.

"But just during practice," he told her. "Trust me. It'll make you a better player."

"But Dad—"

"C'mon, Kari, don't argue with me. Believe me, it'll work."

Karilyn didn't doubt it. But that wasn't the problem. She couldn't imagine anything more humiliating than going to practice with her ponytail tied to her jersey. She couldn't believe that her father would make her do anything so embarrassing. She tried arguing, but it was no use. Once her father made up his mind about something, he very rarely changed it.

Most parents wouldn't have been as demanding as Karilyn's dad. But he had once been a successful high school coach. He had coached all of Karilyn's older brothers and sisters and he knew how to make a good player. Basketball was almost as important to him as church or family.

But to Karilyn, basketball was just a game. She had tears in her eyes as she went to practice, her ponytail tied to her jersey.

Karilyn's father only wanted what was best for her. He only wanted to help improve her game. And most adults are the same way. They push you and push you to do your best because they want you to reach your potential. They want you to be the best you can.

But there are two problems with that. Sometimes their expectations are higher than you are comfortable with. And sometimes their goals are not the same as yours.

Besides that, it's not unusual to have adults pushing you to excel in several areas at once. Think about it. Your mother wants you on the honor roll. Your coach wants you to score twenty points a game. Your Scoutmaster wants you to earn your Eagle by your next birthday. Your boss needs you to work an extra night every week. And every teacher on your schedule assigns homework as if his or hers is the only class you have.

Whew!

It's a wonder more kids don't have ulcers.

Angie Black is a friend of mine who's in the ninth grade. An excellent student, she takes honors classes in biology and English and she plays saxophone in the school stage band three mornings a week before school. She also takes piano lessons, saxophone lessons, and ballet lessons (her mother insisted). In the fall she plays on the school volleyball team and in the spring she runs cross country. As if that's not enough, she also manages to squeeze in time for church meetings, family activities, and homework.

Sound like a lot?

It is! She came into my classroom one day after school looking sad and tired.

"Hard day?" I asked.

She nodded. "There's just so much going on. I don't feel like it ever stops."

Angie enjoyed most of the things she did (although she *did* wish she could quit ballet). But trying to stay current—and good—in so many things was draining both her energy and her enthusiasm.

There are times when the same thing might happen to you.

Believe it or not, a little pressure is actually good for you. It motivates you and sparks your creativity. It keeps you happy, productive, and healthy.

But too much pressure creates stress you don't

need. It can affect your physical, emotional, *and* mental health. Sometimes it can build to the point that you spend days feeling sad, worried, lonely, and miserable.

The sad thing is that most adults don't realize what they're putting you through. A teacher may schedule a big test, never realizing that half the teachers in the school are having tests the same day. A coach might decide to have an extra practice or two every week, forgetting that you still have to make time for your part-time job.

So when the adults in your life start expecting too much from you, and when life gets to be too demanding, here's what you should do.

First, *learn to be honest.*

People will never know how you feel about things unless you tell them. So if you don't want to be on the honor roll, say so. If you can't handle piano lessons three times a week, speak up. If you can't work every single night, tell your boss.

Travis, a friend of mine, is the youngest of seven children in a music-oriented family. He started piano lessons when he was seven and he often sings in church with his brothers and sisters.

Besides that, everyone in his family plays the violin. His brothers and sisters all began taking lessons at the age of ten, and they each played in the school orchestra. They were good, too. Travis's family was known for producing great violinists.

The trouble was that Travis wanted to be a drummer.

"Everybody laughed when I mentioned it," he told me. "After all, we had violins all over the house. And drums and violins don't mix that well."

Still, Travis wasn't going to give up. He was set on being a drummer. But although he didn't want to play the violin, he didn't want to hurt anyone's feelings, either. After all, the violin was an important family instrument.

Then one night, as the family was singing together during family home evening, Travis asked an interesting question.

"What would happen," he asked, "if the Osmond Brothers all sang bass?"

Everybody laughed, and they quickly agreed that they wouldn't have made a very interesting group. But Travis wasn't finished.

"Well, suppose everyone in the Tabernacle Choir sang bass?"

Again, everyone laughed. And again they agreed it wouldn't make for an interesting choir (except, his brother noted, for all of the women basses).

Travis continued. "And what if everyone in the Royal Philharmonic played the violin?"

By now everyone realized that Travis had something on his mind, and they asked him to make his point. So, standing just as tall as he could, he said, "Variety is good. And I think it's time we had a drummer in this family."

Everybody laughed. But in the end, they agreed with him. In a family where everybody plays the violin, Travis got to be a drummer.

Remember that especially with your parents, speaking up won't always make a difference. There are going to be times when you'll have to bite the bullet and do what they want. *You* might be comfortable with a C- in Spanish, but chances are your mother won't be.

Even so, people will never know how you feel unless you tell them. So speak up! Share your goals. Be open and honest about your feelings and priorities.

Second, *learn how to compromise.*

No matter how much you speak up, there will be times when your parents, teachers, and employers will simply lay down the law. When that happens, try offering a compromise.

I have a neighbor named Heather whose parents desperately wanted her to be on the honor roll every term. So Heather made a suggestion.

"I know grades are important to you," she said, trying to be as diplomatic as possible. "But studying takes up a lot of my time. If I get on the honor roll, would you let me quit piano lessons?"

Her parents exchanged glances. They thought piano was important, too.

"Well, then, what if I quit clogging?"

Her parents frowned, but this time they agreed.

It's normal for parents to want you to be head cheerleader, first-chair clarinet, Laurel president, *and* school valedictorian. But all of that might be too much for you. So if your parents feel strongly about your being valedictorian, see if you can't be second-chair clarinet for a while.

Remind them that, after all, you're still a teenager. You still have time to become perfect.

Third, *prove that you're serious about the goals that are important to you.*

My friend Kyle desperately wanted to take karate lessons. But his parents said no, pointing out that they had to hound him to keep up in gymnastics.

"It's not the same," he told them. "Taking gymnastics was *your* idea. Karate is something *I* want to do."

After much discussion, his parents finally relented. But with one condition: "You have to keep up in gymnastics."

Kyle agreed. And he turned out to be a natural at karate. He learned fast and quickly earned his first belt. At home he practiced his techniques over and over again. Before long he was even teaching many of the younger students.

Kyle proved that karate wasn't just a passing fad with him. He was serious about it. And good. He was working to become even better.

After several months, his parents even allowed him to drop gymnastics so he could concentrate on his karate. (The funny thing is that by then, Kyle didn't want to quit gymnastics. He realized that it was helping him to stay loose and flexible for karate.)

I have another friend named Brandon who wanted a bench press for Christmas. But his parents worried that after the first week or two it would sit unused in the basement for the rest of the year. Brandon persisted, however, so they compromised by giving him a barbell and a few weights. Brandon went right to work, organizing a weekly workout schedule and sticking to it. He was so dependable, and made such good use of the equipment he *did* have, that his parents gave him the bench press for his birthday.

When adults learn that you're serious about your goals, when they see that your interests are not just passing fads, they'll be more supportive of them. And many times they'll be more willing to ease up on some of *their* goals for you.

Fourth, *be yourself.*

I think the worst thing that could ever happen is having a brother or sister who's on the verge of becoming the first teenage brain surgeon. Or the next Mozart. Suddenly everyone is comparing the two of you and expecting you to be just as smart. Or just as talented.

I know one young woman whose older sister earned A's all through junior and senior high. But even though Amber was a good student too, top grades didn't come quite so easily for her. Especially in math and English.

Amber felt so much pressure to excel, in fact, that

she finally gave up trying. She knew she could never measure up to her sister, so she simply quit trying. For several weeks she went to math class with nothing more than a reading book.

Finally a wise school counselor stepped in. He convinced Amber that she didn't have to compete with anyone but herself. He told her that it was okay to simply be herself. He convinced her that she was successful as long as she was doing the best she could.

The same thing applies to you. The fact that your father was an All-America quarterback doesn't mean that you have to be. And the fact that your brainy sister can multiply complex polynomials in her head doesn't mean that you have to.

All you have to be is yourself. The only person you ever need to compete with is you. Don't waste time comparing yourself with your brothers, sisters, parents, or friends. Instead, be satisfied with being yourself. Set realistic goals, and be happy when you accomplish them.

Finally, *learn how to handle stress.*

As you get older, you'll notice that problems have the nasty habit of occurring all at once. There will be times when your car breaks down, the computer eats your research paper, your brother spills chocolate on your new dress, and your parents get after you for not doing your chores.

All in the same day!

There will be times when the pressures of life build up all at once and you'll feel like a dam ready to burst.

Keep in mind that stress is a fact of life, and the sooner you learn to manage it, the happier you'll be. One way is to find a healthy release. Get into racquetball, for instance. Or jogging. Or dancing. Or just walking around the block. Anything that will get your heart beating.

It also helps to take time out once in a while to put things in perspective. Take a walk in the woods or listen to your favorite album.

And don't be afraid to talk things out. Find friends who are willing to listen to your problems. Or make an appointment with the school counselor. Sometimes just being able to talk and bring things out in the open will make many of your problems easier to deal with.

It's natural for adults to want you to be your best. But when their expectations become too high, be honest about it. Work together to set good, realistic goals that you can both be comfortable with. Compromise when you can, and prove that you're serious about the goals you *do* set. Be yourself, and learn to manage stress.

Not only will life become easier to deal with, but you'll be healthier and happier too!

Tips to Remember

- Be honest about your priorities. Learn to speak up about things that put too much pressure in your life. Say no to commitments that add unneeded stress and worry.

- If you *have* to make the honor roll this term (and if that's going to be tough), see if there's some activity you can drop to help free up your time. (You could ask permission to skip mowing the lawn or washing the dishes, but that probably won't work.)

- Be serious about the goals you set for yourself. If you want to take drum lessons, work hard to be a good drummer. If you give up band, gymnastics, or piano to play soccer, be sure you become the best soccer player you can.

- Be yourself. Don't go around comparing yourself with your family or friends. Instead, develop your own identity. Remember that as long as you're doing the best you can, you're doing fine!

- Learn how to handle stress. Make pressure work *for* you instead of against you. Find hobbies like biking, swimming, racquetball, and jogging that not only help release the tension that builds up during the week but that also give you activities to look forward to. Sometimes just thinking about an upcoming adventure is enough to pull you through the tough times.

6

THERE'S A COWGIRL IN THE HALLWAY!

Dealing with Rules

Cordell Mulcady had a look of terror in his eyes as he ran through the sagebrush. "Hurry!" he shouted. "We're not going to make it!"

He didn't have to remind me. I was already running as fast as I could, frantically trying to button up the front of my Scout shirt as I went. Camp flag ceremony was about to start, and I didn't dare be late.

I lowered my head and ran harder, passing Cordy and reaching the flagpoles just in the nick of time.

Cordy and I were spending the summer working at Boy Scout camp. One of my best friends in the world, he was a lifeguard; and I ran the camp rifle range.

It was great work. We spent hours every day swimming, shooting, boating, hiking around the lake, and hunting for arrowheads. And we often stayed up late hunting crayfish or telling stories around troop camp-fires.

About the only thing that we *didn't* like was the staff flag ceremony that began promptly at seven o'clock every morning. Anyone who was late or out of uniform had to wash dishes after every meal for the rest of the day.

One morning I woke up so late I didn't have time to find my official Boy Scout shirt. Panicking at the thought of washing dishes all day, I grabbed my jacket, snapping up the front as I dashed through the sage-brush and hoping no one would notice. The only prob-lem was that I had to snap the jacket all the way up to my neck to hide the fact that I wasn't wearing a shirt underneath. Then, during uniform inspection, the camp program director stopped right in front of me.

"Good morning, Shane," he said with a knowing smile.

"Good morning, Hal," I answered, feeling suddenly warm despite the fact that I wasn't entirely dressed.

"Are you wearing your neckerchief today?"

"It's around my collar," I answered truthfully, pic-turing in my mind my shirt and neckerchief both folded together somewhere back in my tent.

"May I see it?"

I was had. Everyone laughed as I trudged off to help the cook.

I never did like that rule much. As a matter of fact, I didn't like the staff flag ceremony at all. As a staff, we raised the flag together every morning. But as soon as we were finished we took it right back down so we could raise it again during the campwide flag cere-mony an hour later.

I thought it was pretty silly. But then the world is full of rules, and many of them are even sillier than that. I know a young woman named Christy, for instance, who plays on her high school's volleyball team. As an incentive to play their best, every time they lose a game the players have to wear their sweaty uniforms in practice for the rest of the week.

"We can't wash them until we win a game," Christy said. "It's dis*gusting*."

Christy didn't think it made much sense, but you probably already know that something doesn't need to make sense to become a rule.

When I was in junior high, I had a teacher who used to write our names on the board when we acted up in class. If we didn't settle down he'd put a check by our name, and then another, and another until we finally settled down. Having our name on the board was a warning. But if we got a check, we had to stay twenty-two seconds after class.

Twenty-two seconds?

That was strange. But if we got *two* checks, we had to stay for *sixty-three* seconds.

I thought that was really weird. It made me curious enough that one day I asked my teacher about it.

"Why do we have to stay for twenty-two seconds?" I asked. "Why not thirty seconds? Or a minute?"

Mr. Riffle just smiled. "Because it *bugs* people," he said.

Well, as I said, it's a rule. It doesn't have to make sense.

Now, you probably come across some pretty silly rules once in a while, too. How you deal with them will affect your standing with the adults who set them, so it's important that you keep these tips in mind.

First, if you run up against a rule you don't like, *try to understand the reason behind it.*

Sometimes there are good reasons for what seem like even the dumbest rules. And when you know what those reasons are, the rules are often easier to live with.

When I was in eighth grade, our basketball coach had a silly way of having us practice foul shooting. We'd line up and take turns shooting a single shot. As soon as the team missed three shots in a row, we had to turn and run a lap at full blast around the gym. Then we'd start over.

It was fun at first. But after two or three laps the novelty wore off.

One day, after our fourth and fifth trip around the court (we weren't the world's best foul shooters), one of my friends started to complain.

"This is so *dumb*," he muttered.

Unfortunately, the coach overheard and blew his whistle.

"I know you don't like this drill," he said as soon as we'd huddled up. "And you don't need to know the reasons for everything we do. But I'll tell you why we're doing this."

The coach then explained that the drill put pressure on us, helping to simulate real game situations.

"But why do we have to run?" someone asked.

The coach shrugged. "Think about what it's like in a game. You're racing up and down the court. Then you get fouled. You don't have time to stop and get a drink and catch your breath. You have to get right up on the line and shoot. You have to learn to shoot foul shots when you're hot and tired and out of breath."

It made sense. We didn't like running the drill any more than we did before, but we quit complaining about it. We knew why we were doing it and we knew it was good for us.

So if there's a rule in your life that you don't like, find out why it's there.

A word of caution here: many adults are sensitive about their rules. So don't just barge up and demand to know *why* you have to do something. Instead, be tactful. Wait for the right time. Then ask about the rule in a nonthreatening way.

Second, *learn how to deal with rules you don't agree with.*

Many people simply ignore rules they don't like. Others rebel. But if you go about it in the right way, there are many rules you can actually have changed.

I did my student teaching at a high school where kids had a hard time getting to class. At almost any time during the day you could look out in the hall and see about as many kids there as you could in class.

Then the principal came up with an idea. Once or twice each day he came on over the intercom and said, "All right, teachers . . . *roundup!*"

At that point, all of the teachers who weren't in the middle of a lesson, and all of the secretaries, custodians, and administrators, would link arms and march down the halls, herding in front of them everyone not in class. Students trying to escape would turn a corner, only to find another wall of teachers closing in.

The teachers herded everyone down the halls and into the cafeteria, where the principal was waiting with a clipboard. He jotted down each person's name and his or her reason for being in the hall; then he assigned penalties.

Sound like something you'd see on a TV sitcom? It was! Not many teachers enjoyed the routine. And hardly any of the students did. Most people thought it was a pretty immature way of dealing with high school students.

And that's when the real problems started.

Many kids thought the idea of a roundup was so ridiculous that they openly rebelled. They started showing up to school dressed as cowboys (one girl I know even came dressed with chaps and a lariat), then deliberately stood around in the halls just hoping for another roundup.

What started as a simple problem became so bad that several students were eventually suspended.

Fortunately, a few of the school's more level-headed students took a more positive approach. They started a petition, had people write letters, and made a presentation to the faculty council. They succeeded in having the roundups stopped.

It's easy to rebel against rules you don't like. But learning to deal with unfair rules constructively won't just help you now. It's good training for when you run into laws you don't agree with as an adult.

I live near a junior high school that had a policy against chewing gum and eating candy. The students all begged for a change, but the administration worried that the halls would soon be littered with wrappers.

One year the student council decided it wasn't going to take no for an answer. They talked the principal into giving them a chance. They convinced him to change the rule on a trial basis. And if, after a week, the halls became trashy, they said, he was welcome to change his mind.

As it turned out, not only did the halls stay clean but that same school has pop and candy machines in the halls now, too.

If you go about it in the right way, there are many rules that you can have changed. So if there's a rule that's cramping your style, don't rebel. Instead, take a positive approach and see if you can have it changed.

Third, *don't wait to challenge a rule until it's too late.* When I was in high school, I had a teacher who didn't tolerate students who were late to class. She was so strict, in fact, that if we walked in after the bell, she refused to accept our work for that day.

That may seem rather harsh, but that was her rule. Many students didn't agree with it, but no one did anything about it. Not, that is, until my friend Tyler was late to class one day. We had an important essay due, and when Tyler tried to turn his in, Miss Callahan refused to accept it.

Now, Tyler was a good student. He was working toward a scholarship, and he wasn't late to class on purpose. Having Miss Callahan refuse his essay was sure to hurt his grade.

Tyler was so upset that he, his parents, and Miss Callahan all ended up in the principal's office shouting at one another.

The real problem was that whether the rule was fair or not, Tyler knew what it was. And he knew the consequences too. By the time he chose to do anything about getting the rule changed, it was too late.

I know another teacher who does not allow students to work on assignments from other classes during his class. And that's reasonable. But if you get caught working on something else, he'll take it away and he won't return it. Once again, that might seem wrong to you. But if you don't agree with it, don't wait until you have one of your assignments torn up before you try talking to the teacher about it.

If there's a rule that's threatening to ruin your life, don't wait until you break it before trying to get it changed. If you do, you're not likely to get very far.

Finally, *remember that there are always going to be rules that you can't do anything about.* You can get everyone in the neighborhood to protest and your parents *still* might not let you date until you're sixteen. You can appeal to the Supreme Court and *still* have to take two years of math in high school.

That's the way it is sometimes. So when you run into a rule that's just not going to change, grit your teeth and learn to live with it.

It's important for you to be a good sport here. If your parents won't let you date until you're sixteen (and if there's no chance that they're going to change their minds) don't spend the next six months whining about it. You won't accomplish anything. But you *will* strain your relationship with your parents.

Most rules exist for good reasons. Many are actually for your own good. But when you run into one that isn't, don't rebel. Instead, take a positive approach to the problem. Work constructively to have it changed.

This approach will not only make things easier for you now but also will give you experience that will help you during your whole life.

Tips to Remember

- When you come across a rule you don't agree with, find out if there's a reason behind it. Obviously, someone thinks it's important. And who knows? Once you know why it's there, you might even agree with it.

- If you come across a rule that you think is unfair, don't rebel. Instead, take a positive approach. Work through proper channels to have the rule changed or modified.

- If you run up against a rule you don't agree with, get working on it *now!* Don't wait until it gets you in trouble before you try changing it.

- As you follow these tips, keep in mind that many adults are sensitive about their rules. So be diplomatic. Don't just barge up and demand to know why you have to follow certain rules. Don't simply insist that an unfair rule be changed. Instead, wait for the proper time, then conduct your business in a nonthreatening way.

- Be sensitive to those rules that can't be changed. Be a good sport and put up with them as best you can. You're going to run into them for your whole life, so get used to living with them.

7

I'VE BEEN GROUNDED UNTIL I'M TWENTY-ONE!

Dealing with Punishment

If you've ever been punished for something, then you know what this chapter is all about.

In all of your dealings with adults, there's nothing that can strain your relationship faster than being punished. If your parents ground you, you don't speak to them for a week. If your coach puts you on the bench, you think he's a jerk. And if your favorite teacher keeps you after class, she goes from being your biggest hero to your worst enemy.

Which isn't always fair. Sometimes your parents, coaches, and teachers are only doing what they have to do. They may not have any other choice.

I remember reading about a high school quarterback who was caught drinking a can of beer at a school picnic. Not only was drinking against the law, but it was against team rules, too. And he was suspended from the team for the rest of the season.

The boy's father was so mad that he went right to the school with a list of eight more football players who were also drinking at the picnic. They were also suspended for the rest of the season.

Now, there's not many teams that could lose nine players and survive. And that's one of the worst things about punishment. It often affects innocent people. In this case, it was impossible to punish the nine boys without punishing the rest of the team too.

But the interesting thing was that no one blamed the boys for what they did. Instead, everyone was angry with the coaches and administrators for suspending them.

When things like this happen to you, don't blame the coach! If you're late to class and have to spend time there after school, don't be mad at your teacher. If you forget to do your chores and get grounded, don't blame your parents.

After all, the adults probably don't like the situation any more than you do. It's a good bet that the coach doesn't want you off the team. It's easier for teachers to be friends than enemies. And your parents certainly don't want you moping around the house for the next week.

I teach at a junior high school and live in the same neighborhood as many of my students. A lot of the neighbor kids end up in my classes, and I know most of these kids pretty well. I take a lot of them water skiing, and I often go hiking and camping with the Scouts. So by the time they get into my class, we're usually pretty good pals.

Now, that might sound like fun, but it's not. At least, not for me. That's because even the best kids break rules once in a while. And that puts me in a difficult position. If I get after them for it, they get mad at me for not being their "friend." But if I let them get away with it, I'm not being fair to the rest of the class.

When my sister was a teenager, she once went toilet-papering houses with her friends. Someone called the police, and before the kids had finished the first house a squad car pulled up. Everybody ran, but my sister (only *my* sister would do this) jumped over a hedge and broke her leg (she got "busted" in more ways than one).

Well, the real problem was that my dad was a policeman. And the officer who caught my sister not only worked under him but also was a good friend of the family. He chewed my sister out until she was in tears.

He wasn't so mad about the toilet papering. But he was angry that she put *him* in a position where he had to get *her* in trouble.

The point of all this simply is that some adults don't like dishing out punishment any more than you enjoy receiving it. But sometimes they just don't have a choice. At times like these, don't blame them for it.

One of the worst things about punishment is that it's not always fair. Especially when you're not at fault. How often have you been in a school class, for instance, and had your teacher punish the whole class for something that only one or two kids were doing?

Or—even worse—how often have you had the class clown poke you, push you, or maybe shoot you with a spitwad when the teacher's back was turned? And as soon as you turn around to make him stop the teacher gets mad at *you?*

It happens. And it's not fair. But the worst thing you can do is argue about it. After all, your teacher, mother, or boss is probably upset. And arguing is just going to make things worse.

So here's a better idea. If you ever get in trouble for

something you didn't do, *wait until everyone has calmed down before doing anything.* This is hard to do. But talking back or arguing will only make things worse.

I know a young woman named Melanie whose science class was so noisy one day that the teacher assigned everyone a typed, two thousand-word report due the next day.

Everybody moaned and groaned. Especially the kids who hadn't been noisy. So the teacher responded by making the report three thousand words.

Melanie could have fussed like everyone else. But instead, she waited until after class, waited until the teacher was by himself, then went up for a talk. She showed him how much work she had done that day and said, "I was really working hard. And I wasn't talking. I don't think I should have to do the report."

Her teacher agreed. He gave her a slip excusing her from the assignment.

I have another friend who was taking woodshop. Unfortunately, there were two boys in the class who were constantly breaking rules and disrupting the class. Because of them, the teacher made the whole class remain in the classroom, reading the textbook and writing reports.

Worse than that was the fact that everyone was being graded on their woodshop projects, but no one was given any time to work on them!

So after two or three days, my friend Nick and a couple of his classmates went in to see the teacher.

"We're doing everything you ask us to do," they told him. "And we're not causing the problems. We deserve to work on our projects." The teacher saw their point and immediately changed his tactics. He quit punishing the whole class and zeroed in on just those students who were breaking the rules.

Don't forget that punishment is stressful on every-body. It causes as much tension to the person doing the punishing as the person being punished. So if you don't deserve a punishment, don't fan the fire! Wait for a better time and place, then present proof of your in-nocence.

Besides being punished for things you didn't do, there might be times when you get slapped with pun-ishments that seem unreasonable. In the heat of the moment, some adults might blow up and dock your grade fifty thousand points, ground you until you're twenty-one, or maybe even fire you.

I know a young man named Tim who one day left his seat in the middle of his biology class. His teacher (probably stressed out to begin with) blew up.

"I want you out of my class!" he yelled. "Now! I don't care where you go or what you do. But I don't want to see you again until you have a slip to transfer out of here!"

There's no question that the teacher was being un-reasonable. And maybe you've had a similar experi-ence. But believe it or not, when most adults blow up they often feel bad about it later. After they've cooled off and their blood pressure has returned to normal, they usually realize that they've been unreasonable. And they often wish that they'd acted differently.

And *that's* when you want to approach them. If you were in the wrong, admit it, but explain that you think the punishment is a little harsh. You might even go so far as to suggest a more reasonable penalty.

This way, not only do you stand a good chance of reducing an unreasonable punishment, but a calm dis-cussion will put the two of you back on speaking terms. You'll feel better about one another. And you'll be well on your way to being friends again.

When I was working at Boy Scout camp, at one

point we had a camp director who was mean, bossy, and short-tempered.

And those were his good points!

One day one of the boys on the staff was trying to get into the swimming pool area when he broke the handle on the door. The rest of us did not know who had done it, so the boss banned the whole staff from the pool.

That made us mad!

After all, we worked hard, and going swimming after hours was one of the few things we could do around camp to relax and have a little fun. I was so mad, in fact, that I stormed into the supply room, got a new doorknob, took a screwdriver, and spent my whole dinner break fixing the door.

I did the right thing, but I did it in the wrong way and for the wrong reasons. I ended up in more trouble than I was in in the first place.

Finally, though, I went to the camp director and talked things over with him. We worked things out. And even though we never did figure out who broke the door, we finally got to use the pool again.

Nothing will challenge your ability to survive in a grown-up's world as much as dealing with punishment. So if you deserve what you're getting (and be honest about it) don't blame an adult for punishing you. If you don't deserve to be punished, don't fuel the fire by arguing or talking back. Wait until everyone's tempers have cooled off, then try to work things out reasonably.

Not only will you avoid a lot of stress, but the experience will bring you closer together.

Tips to Remember

- If you really want to avoid problems, don't do anything that's going to get you punished in the first place. (Don't put adults in the position of *having* to punish you. If you're close to an adult, don't ever make him decide between your friendship and doing what he has to do.)

- If staying out of trouble is impossible (no one's perfect), don't blame the person who has to punish you. He probably doesn't like it any better than you do. And blaming him for *your* mistake will only strain your relationship even more.

- When someone gets after you for something that's not your fault, stay calm. Bite your lip if you have to, but don't argue or talk back. Instead, wait until everyone has calmed down and *then* try to work things out.

- If you get hit with a punishment that's unreasonable, stay calm! Most adults will come to their senses after they've cooled off a bit. They'll probably even feel bad about what they've done. So give the adult a chance to calm down, *then* see if you can work things out.

- Don't hold grudges. No matter what happens, be mature enough to let things pass. Even when you've been treated unfairly, be big enough to let it go. Grudges will only sour your attitude and make things worse.

8

A FRIEND NAMED EDWEIRD

Getting Adults to Accept Your Friends

Donny George was one of the best friends I ever had.

Fifteen years old, he had eyes the color of Windex, and braces that he flashed around as if they were his most prized possession. I first met him while working at Boy Scout camp, and we ended up working together for a couple of years. He was one of the reasons I kept going back year after year.

One time I was busy cutting down weeds at the rifle range when Donny came running up the hill. "Hal sent me to find you," he said, puffing for breath. "They need you down at the lodge for something."

I groaned. I still had another hour or so of work to do on the weeds, and I didn't have time to leave. But I knew that Hal wouldn't send for me if he didn't have to, so I put down my tools and took off.

When I returned an hour later, the weeds had all been cut.

Donny just shrugged when I asked him about it. "They needed to be cut," he said. "So I cut 'em."

That's the kind of friend he was. He made every day fun for me. He made me feel important. He made me feel needed. He made me feel as if I were someone special.

Most important, he brought out the best in me.

Friends can do that for you. They can take your worst days and make them your best ones. They can make you feel good. They can bring out the best in you.

Unfortunately, there may be times when your friends don't quite hit it off with your parents. Maybe the friends have long hair or wear funny clothes. Perhaps they listen to strange music or drive souped-up cars.

Whatever the reason, it's never easy when your parents don't like your friends.

I once wrote a book that featured a character named Edweird. His real name was Edward, but he was so strange that no one ever called him that. Instead, it was always Ed*weird*. He was the town hood; his hair was long and greasy, and all the kids in town were afraid of him.

He was one of my favorite characters.

But what most people don't realize is that I didn't make him up. I really did know a person called Edweird. He wasn't a hood like the character in my book, but he was strange nevertheless.

Now, how would you like to tell your parents that your best friend is a kid named Edweird? Knowing your friends like they do, they might not be surprised. Even so, it's important that your parents learn to accept your friends. Otherwise they'll resist letting you spend time with them.

If your parents don't like your friends, try to figure out why. If it's because your friends are a bad influence—if they keep you from doing well in school or if they expose you to drugs, drinking, or immorality—then your parents are right. *Real* friends are people who build you up. Those who pressure you to travel in wrong directions are not good.

But if it's simply because they look or act a little different—if it's just because your parents don't understand them—that's okay. It's possible to work things out.

The first thing you have to do is let your parents get to know them.

For many young people, home is the last place they want to hang out when they're with their friends. So they spend all their time away, never letting their parents have a chance to see who they're hanging out with.

But if you really want your parents to like and accept your friends, you've got to let your parents get to know them. The next time one of your stranger friends comes by, then, introduce her to your parents. Then stick around the house for a little while. Let your parents see what she's really like.

I used to work with a seventeen-year-old girl named Stacy. She had a friend named Cal whom her parents didn't like very much. The problem was that Cal had an earring, his hair was a little long, and he dressed like someone out of an MTV video.

But he was also one of the smartest boys Stacy knew. He earned straight A's in school and his schedule was crammed with AP classes. Cal had a wonderful sense of humor, and he was the most creative boy Stacy had ever dated. When they went out he didn't just take her to a movie and out for pizza like most boys did. He went out of his way to be original and to make every date a special event.

Stacy knew that her parents would like Cal if they just got to know him. So she always arranged to have Cal pick her up about half an hour earlier than he needed to. This way they could visit with her parents for a while before buzzing off.

One day Cal and Stacy planned to go to a picnic. Cal came over and found Stacy's mother getting ready to paint the family room, only she was having trouble taping the windows, doorknobs, and door frames.

"Here," Cal said. "My dad's a painter. I have to tape for him all the time."

Then, jumping right in, he taped up everything in sight. He and Stacy were an hour late to their picnic, but they didn't mind. In that hour, Stacy's mother got to see the real Cal. She not only saw the thoughtful, helpful side, but she also got to visit with him and experience his personality firsthand. She was able to see him the way Stacy did.

The next week Stacy's parents invited Cal over for Sunday dinner.

So let your parents get to know your friends. Let them see what they're really like. Give them a chance to see your friends' good points.

Sometimes parents get uptight about friends simply because there's such an aura of mystery about them. They don't know anything about them, and the less they know, the more they worry. Part of this is because many teenagers are so worried about their privacy that they become *too* secretive.

Think about it. When you come home after being out with your friends and your parents ask where you've been, how often do you say, "Oh, just around"? Or after an hour-long phone call, have you ever told your parents you were just talking about "stuff"?

By giving such vague answers you may think that you're preserving your privacy. But what you're really doing is creating an aura of mystery that makes your parents worry.

So eliminate the mystery. When your parents ask where you've been, tell them! You don't need to give them a minute-by-minute, mile-by-mile travelogue. But satisfy their curiosity a little. Try saying something like this: "We went over to Casey's for a while, and then over to the Burger Barn for a milkshake." Or this: "Lisa needed a new pair of 501s, so we went to the mall for a couple of hours." Or this: "Mike's brother just got a new motorcycle; we've been trying to help him fix it up."

By telling your parents where you're going and what you're doing, you accomplish two things. You ease their curiosity, which keeps them from worrying so much. And as long as you're telling the truth and they know it, your parents will realize that your friends are safe to be with. They'll learn that when you're with Jane or Heather or Mike you're not smoking, drinking, or going to wild parties. They'll know that you're probably studying, shopping, or working on old cars.

A word of caution here: you have to be honest. If you tell your parents that you spent the evening at the Pizza Palace, and they later find out that you didn't, they'll quit trusting you. And they'll be twice as worried about your friends as they were before.

So be open about what you do with your friends, but be honest.

It also helps to be open about the things you and your friends talk about. If you come in late and find your parents still up, go sit with them for a minute before going to bed. And try saying something like this: "Mike was just telling me about his little brother, Jeff. He plays on a Junior Jazz basketball team and he hasn't scored a basket all season. Then, last Saturday he got the ball on an inbounds pass and ran all the way down the court for a layup—in *the wrong basket!*"

Or you might say something like this: "Marcie is so mad at her science teacher. Yesterday two boys started goofing around so he made the whole class do extra work. She hates him *so* bad . . ."

Or if one of your friends tells you a funny joke, share it with your parents and tell them where you heard it.

When your parents begin to understand the sort of things you and your friends talk about, they have less and less to wonder about. And worry about.

I've already told you about my friend Edweird. I had another friend named Steve who used to go home every night and tell story after story about him. Every night it was, "You should have seen what Edweird brought for lunch today," or "You should have seen Edweird trying out for the school play this afternoon . . . he is *such* a dozer!"

Steve's parents heard so much about Ed that they actually *wanted* to meet him. It got to the point that they were saying, "When are you going to bring Edweird home so we can meet him?"

You have to remember that even though Ed was the original Mr. Strange, he really was a nice kid. He was always doing something off the wall, but it was never anything harmful or dangerous. And everybody liked him. So even though you might think a person named Edweird ought to be avoided, Steve's parents knew he was harmless long before they ever met him.

Your parents will be the same way. No matter how funny your friends look, if they're really harmless your parents will learn to accept them. So talk about them! Let your parents feel they really know them.

This works in reverse, too. I used to date a girl whose father was a high school football coach. I knew enough about coaches that I was nervous about meeting him, and whenever I went to see Jill I prayed that her father wouldn't be home.

But Jill loved her father and she let me know it. She talked about him enough that it wasn't long before I realized that he wasn't a mean, rough 'n' tough hunk of meat who ate nails for breakfast. Instead, he was a man with a wacky sense of humor who loved to hunt and fish and who tied his own fishing flies.

Suddenly, instead of being afraid of the man, I was anxious to meet him. Jill had told me all about his gun collection, and I wanted to see it.

Your parents will be the same way. When they learn why you like certain people, they'll find it easier to accept them. They'll feel better about the time you spend together.

And who knows? Parents get so worried about kids who waste time watching TV that if they know you've got good friends, they might actually *want* you to spend more time with them.

Here's a final suggestion. If you really want your parents to accept your friends—and if you want to score a few points with your parents while you're at it—try this. The next time you go somewhere with your pals, invite your little brother or sister to go along.

Now, I know what you're thinking. Half the reason you spend time with your friends is to escape your siblings. But look at it this way. Your parents will appreciate the time you spend with your brothers and sisters. But more important, your brothers and sisters will be able to testify how "cool" your friends are.

Give it a try. It works.

Good friends can have a wonderful effect on you. They can inspire you, motivate you, and pull you through tough times. Friends are important to being a successful teenager, so it's vital that your parents like the ones you choose.

So let your parents get to know them. Hang around the house once in a while just to let your parents get to know them better. Be open and honest about the things you do together, and let your parents in on the things you and your friends talk about.

As you do, your parents will begin to see your friends through *your* eyes. They might even end up liking them as much as you do!

Tips to Remember

- Let your parents get to know your friends. Stick around the house for a few minutes before taking off for the movie. Or if you're just going to play catch, study, or watch TV together, do it at *your* house once in a while.

- When parents have to wonder what you're up to, they start to worry. So remove the mystery. Let them know where you're going and what you're doing when you're with your friends. Remember to *be honest!*

- Share your conversations. Tell your parents the sort of things your friends talk about. Share the jokes and stories they tell you. The more you talk about your friends, the more your parents will feel they know them.

- Let your little brothers or sisters tag along with you once in a while. Your parents will appreciate it. Your brothers and sisters will appreciate it. And they'll help convince your parents how "awesome" your friends really are.

9

CHIPMUNKS, SUNFLOWER SEEDS, AND THE COSBY SHOW

Getting Along with Parents

My dad often asked me to do strange things. But this time I was sure he had to be joking. I held the telephone a little closer to my ear.

"You want me to buy you what?"

"A hundred pounds of sunflower seeds," he repeated, sounding as calm as if he were asking me to pick up a loaf of bread or a quart of milk. But a hundred pounds of sunflower seeds? I don't think I've eaten *one* pound during my whole *life*.

"You're sure you want a *hundred* pounds? What are you going to do with that many sunflower seeds?"

"They're for your mother," he told me. "She wants to take them up to the cabin."

Suddenly I understood. My mother. She was into squirrels like some kids are into Teenage Mutant Ninja

Turtles. She had pictures of them hanging in her office and printed on her sweatshirts. She had wooden, plastic, and ceramic sculptures of squirrels scattered all over the house. She even had my little brother etch a picture of one into the window of her car.

And that was just for starters. My dad had a cabin deep in the woods, and my mom was forever scattering seeds and nuts for all the little animals there. Then she'd spend hours watching as they gathered them all up.

I always thought it was a bit strange. But one day I happened to be sitting on the porch of the cabin when a chipmunk scampered up to my chair. It sat up on its hind legs, wrinkled its nose, then darted away. A moment later it was back. It sniffed my shoe, then suddenly ran up my leg, scrambled onto my shoulder, and perched on top of my hat.

I was sitting as still as I could, trying not to laugh, when it jumped off my hat and onto the pages of the book I was reading. It couldn't get traction on the paper and its tiny legs spun like miniature propellers.

It finally leaped to safety and darted into the bushes. And the next minute I was scattering around handfuls of sunflower seeds, hoping it would come back. Suddenly I understood my mother a little bit better. I knew why she enjoyed the little critters so much. So when my dad asked me to pick up a hundred pounds of seeds for her, I was happy to do it.

Now, your parents probably have things about them that make them different too. Sometimes those things can cause conflicts. Your parents might be a little too strict with rules, for instance. Or maybe they're overprotective. And perhaps they insist that you practice the piano an hour and a half every day.

Any of those things might create friction between you.

"All of my friends have parents like the Huxtables on 'The Cosby Show,'" one young woman wailed. "My parents are more like Homer and Marge on 'The Simpsons'!"

Have you ever felt like that? Well, you're not alone. The truth is, no one's parents are perfect. And that's good. (If your parents were perfect, think what everyone would expect of you!)

In church, at school, and especially on TV, you see examples of ideal families. But there's really no such thing. Even families that appear to be "perfect" are sure to have problems.

Your parents, too, are certain to have their little quirks, but they'll make up for them in other ways. The important thing is learning to forgive their faults while focusing on their strengths.

When I was in high school I had a friend named Dana whose father was an alcoholic. He was never abusive, but Dana grew up knowing her father would never sit beside her in church. And she was reluctant to take her friends home, worried that she might embarrass her father by catching him while he was intoxicated.

The wonderful thing about Dana was that she never gave up hope.

"I love my dad," she once told me. "He makes a lot of mistakes. And I feel bad about his problems. But he's still my dad."

I have another friend named Aaron who's the last in a string of nine kids. By the time Aaron was in junior high, his dad was ready to retire. He wasn't interested anymore in things like camping, baseball, and fishing.

Many of Aaron's friends, on the other hand, were the oldest children in their families. That meant their fathers were relatively young and many of them were always willing to jump in the middle of a basketball game, go camping, or umpire a ball game.

Aaron told me that he missed having a father who could coach his ball team or take the Scout troop camping. But he knew that his dad made up for that in other ways.

Aaron's dad was, for instance, one of the most intelligent men I knew. He could talk for hours on the formation of planets and black holes and other things we found fascinating. He even had a scientific explanation for Bigfoot! (How can you not admire a man like that?)

You can find as many faults in your parents as you want. But if you look, you're certain to find as many good points to make up for them. So focus on the things they do right and learn to accept the things they don't.

Remember, too, that because they're not perfect, they're bound to make mistakes in the way they raise you. There's just no way around it. So if they slip up from time to time, don't fly off the handle. Learn to forgive and forget. (And then hope they'll do the same for you.)

And try to be patient with them. It's not easy being a teenager these days, and it's just as tough being a parent. Your parents not only have to worry about how well they're raising you, but they have jobs, church callings, and taxes nagging at them. As if that's not enough, they've got leaky faucets, plugged drain pipes, car payments, bills, and rising insurance rates to keep up with too.

It's a lot to worry about. And even parents who are normally fun, even-tempered, and easygoing might explode once in a while. (Especially when taxes come due, the toilet backs up, and the car breaks down all on the same day.)

So if your mother's or father's temper boils over once in a while, don't take it personally. If it happens on a regular basis, discuss it with your other parent, bishop, or a counselor at school. But otherwise try to understand what's happening in their lives and let it go.

I know a young woman whose father suffers from a chemical imbalance, which makes him moody and short-tempered. The doctor put him on medication for a while, which helped, but caused unpleasant side effects. "He finally stopped taking the medicine," Stephanie told me. "So he still gets mad over little things sometimes. But we all know he's trying, so we don't let it get to us."

That's a good attitude. All parents make mistakes, but they're trying. A father who snaps at you might actually be reacting to a bad day at work. A mother who gets cranky might be showing the strain of a long day. If that's the case, be understanding. Arguing or talking back will only make their bad day worse. And it will just make things worse for you.

Actually, at times like these you can do a lot to ease the situation. Replace the stress and tension they're feeling with love and appreciation.

A teenager named Trish, for instance, told me about a time when her father was in danger of being laid off from work. For weeks he worried about it, and the tension made him grumpy, tired, and depressed. Even the littlest of things would set him off. If Trish didn't do the dishes when she was supposed to, her dad would yell. If someone had the radio on too loud, he would explode. It got so that the kids were almost afraid to go home, worried that they'd get yelled at.

Then one day Trish's older brother Mike called all the kids together. He explained that their father wasn't really angry with them; he was just worried about losing his job. And it was the stress that was causing his bad temper. Mike told them to hang in there and that eventually things would get back to normal.

The next night Trish came home to find her dad sitting in his favorite chair. On impulse she began massaging his shoulders.

"It was weird," Trish told me. "I could feel how tense he was. But after a few minutes he started to relax. And he was happy for the rest of the evening."

A couple of days later, Mike went outside and began raking up the leaves. That wasn't his job, but he knew it had to be done so he decided to take care of it. Trish went to help. Then, when their father came home, he grinned, grabbed a garbage bag, and helped his children bag the leaves.

Gestures like this help keep families together. They prevent many problems from ever happening. And when things do go bad, they put you in a better position to work things out.

Another hint is not to quibble over little things. Maybe your parents want to have family scripture study every morning. Or family home evening once a week. Or family sharing time before dinner. Maybe they like to visit old Aunt Bessie each Sunday and they actually *expect you to go with them!*

You may not like it. But these are just *little things.* It's silly to let something as insignificant as an hour-long trip to the rest home drive a wedge between you and your parents. Remember (you have to keep telling yourself this) that your parents only want the best for the family. And simple things like family home evening and family prayer make them feel they're strengthening the family.

So consider those things your parents do that bug you. When it's something little, give in! Do it and get it over with. It'll be over before you know it. And it will relieve a lot of stress and tension in the family.

A similar idea is to be a peacemaker with your brothers and sisters. If you have siblings who cause a little stress, step in and help. Not only will this relieve tension around the house, but your parents will notice and appreciate the effort. And that appreciation will go a long way in smoothing your own dealings with them.

(As I mentioned in the previous chapter, if you really want to score points, try inviting your little brother or sister along the next time you go somewhere with your friends. There's nothing that warms parents' hearts like seeing their kids being friends and doing things together.)

Finally, don't be afraid to talk. Remember that your parents can't read your mind. If they have hurt your feelings or disappointed you somehow, tell them. If they're neglecting you, tell them. If you need something from them, tell them.

And be specific. Don't generalize by saying things like, "You don't trust me," or "You're not fair." Instead, be as specific as you can. Say things like, "When you nag me about my homework you make me feel like a little kid," or "When you don't let me go out with my friends, it embarrasses me; it makes me feel you don't trust me."

By being specific, you're telling your parents exactly what you need from them. It eliminates the guesswork. It tells them exactly what they need to do to meet your needs.

I have a friend named Summer who desperately wanted a mountain bike for her birthday. But she never said so. Whenever her parents asked her what she wanted, she'd say something like, "It doesn't matter . . . anything is fine."

Inside, Summer hoped her parents would somehow figure out what she wanted. But it didn't happen. And she ended up feeling hurt and disappointed.

Your parents can't read your mind either. So if you need something, don't play games. Don't make them guess. Be specific. Tell them exactly what you want or need.

Another hint is to be positive. Rather than say things like, "I hate it when you don't let me use the car," say, "It'd be great if you'd let me borrow the car more often." Instead of complaining that "you always make me come home too early," say, "I'd feel more grown up if you'd let me stay out a little later."

Making positive statements does two things. It keeps your parents from feeling they're under attack and from becoming defensive. And it tells them exactly what it is you want.

Talking out problems isn't always an easy thing to do, but if you don't, your parents will never know how you feel. Besides, if you keep things bottled up inside, you'll only feel more stress and resentment. And if you don't talk, you and your parents will simply drift farther and farther apart.

(If talking things out is too uncomfortable, try talking with just one of your parents first. Or maybe talk things over with your brothers and sisters, then go to your parents together. You might even think about going to your bishop and inviting him to sit in on your talk.)

Remember, too, that it's just as important to express your feelings when you're happy as when you're not. If your parents do or say something that makes you happy, tell them! After all, parents worry about making mistakes. When they figure they've finally done something right, they're bound to do it again.

No matter what they're like, your parents are the

most important people in your life. You cannot be a successful teenager without them. So look past their hang-ups. Be understanding when the pressures and burdens of life make them gruff, edgy, or cranky. Do what you can to help keep peace around the house.

Most important of all, don't be afraid to talk when problems come up. Be specific and tell them exactly what you need from them. Be positive and let them know when they're doing well.

You'll find that your parents aren't just good partners. They can also make great friends.

Tips to Remember

- Don't compare your parents with others you know. Even parents who seem perfect have their problems. (Remember that the wise, warm, and wonderful parents you always see on TV are just as fictitious as their lovable, huggable, sugar-sweet kids.)

- Learn to appreciate your parents' good points. Look past their faults and appreciate them for the things they do well. Keep in mind that no matter how many mistakes they make, they're probably doing the best they can. Appreciate them for the efforts they make.

- Be patient. Don't get down on your parents if they get a little uptight now and again. Try to understand the pressures and demands that drain their energy and enthusiasm.

- Don't make a big deal out of little things. If your parents want to have family home evening, family prayer, or anything else you might think is silly, don't quibble. Remember that these are just little things. Don't let them drive wedges between you and your parents.

- Help out around the house. Not only will this relieve a lot of stress and tension, but it will also create feelings of love and appreciation. It will prevent many problems from ever happening.

- Talk things out when you have a problem. Be as specific as you can. Make certain your parents know exactly how you feel. Learn to phrase statements positively.

10

THAT'S NO CREATURE, THAT'S MY TEACHER!

Getting Along with Teachers

Heather Rypien looked as if she were going to explode. Her face was red and her eyes blazed with anger. "I *hate* Mr. Owens," she said, slamming her books down on my desk. "I hate him *so* bad!"

I pushed away the assignments I was grading and stood up. "Mr. Owens? Why?"

Heather clenched her eyes and shook her head as if the mere thought of her new English teacher was too painful to bear. "Ooooh!" she said. "He just makes me so mad!"

"But why?"

"Because he's so stupid! Last period we were taking a test. I got up to sharpen my pencil and *he took my test away!*"

"Really?"

"Yes! Can you believe it? He took my test and gave me a zero just for being out of my seat!"

It did sound a little strange. Heather was a bright, enthusiastic ninth grader who had been on the honor roll every term since seventh grade. Purposely breaking class rules was something she just didn't do.

On the other hand, I had been a teacher long enough to know that there had to be two sides to the story. There had to be more going on than Heather was aware of.

"Did you try talking to him about it?" I asked.

"Yes! But he wouldn't listen. He just told me to go back to my seat and sit down!"

I wanted to talk with Heather a little longer, but students were beginning to file in for my next class and we both had to get going. I was thinking about going in to see Mr. Owens after school, but before I could, Heather came skipping back into my room.

"I got things worked out with Mr. Owens," she told me. "I went in to see him and he finally listened to me." She beamed. "He apologized, and he's not even going to make me retake the test."

I was happy everything had worked out. Heather was a good student and I enjoyed having her in my algebra class. And from what I knew of him, Mr. Owens was a good teacher. It was nice to see that one misunderstanding wasn't going to spoil their relationship.

Just as important, Heather proved how easily many problems with teachers can be resolved. In her case, all it took was going in after school to talk things over.

Now, what about you? When you have problems with teachers, do you go home moaning to your friends and family about what jerks teachers are? Or do you honestly try to work things out?

A young woman named Camille was constantly in

trouble with her Spanish teacher. Hardly a day went by that he didn't get after her for something. "He's always picking on me!" she complained. "It's always, 'Camille, get back to work,' or 'Camille, get back in your seat.' If I ever talk in class, he makes me stay after. If I ever ask a question, he makes me sit in the back of the room."

To make matters worse, Camille said that Mr. Adams never got after anyone else but her. (Have you ever felt like that?) No matter who else was talking, Camille was the only one who ever got in trouble.

Things went on that way until the day Mr. Adams gave Camille a zero for talking during a test. And that was the last straw. Grabbing her books, Camille got up and stormed out of the room, calling her teacher a string of colorful names as she left.

Now, if Camille honestly felt that her teacher was picking on her, she should have tried to straighten things out before this happened. She probably didn't feel that she could talk to Mr. Adams about it, but she could have talked to her parents, or a counselor, or the principal.

Letting things go only made things worse. And in the end, it was Camille who got in trouble. (It's not good to call your teacher names in the middle of class!)

Whether you like it or not, when you're in junior and senior high you spend about six hours a day in school. And that's a big chunk of time. In fact, there's a good chance that you spend more time with teachers each day than you spend with your parents.

You *have* to learn to get along with them.

Besides, teachers play an important part in your life. They not only hold the key to your education, but they can also open many of the doors you need to get jobs and scholarships.

Just as important, when you have a good relationship with your teachers you'll prevent many problems from ever happening. So let's look at a couple of ways to do that.

First, *make certain that your teachers know who you are.*

Remember that junior- and senior-high teachers face almost two hundred students every day. So to them you're just one in a sea of faces. You have to set yourself apart from the crowd.

There are a couple of ways to do this. Start by saying hi when you pass them in the hall. And if you happen to pass their room on your way to another class, poke your head in the door once in a while and wave. This might seem silly—and it's hard to do at first—but it works. It sets you apart. And it tells your teachers that you care about them.

Next, *let your teachers get to know you as a person.*

Take time to visit occasionally before and after class. Let them know what you do in your spare time. Tell them what your interests are. If you have a piano recital coming up, give them an invitation. If you write a poem or short story, give them a copy.

This might seem like major-league bowing and scraping, but it's not. In fact, if you're going to spend nine months in a person's class, it's silly not to be on as good terms as possible.

I once taught a student whom I had a hard time reaching. He muddled along doing average work, but he never asked questions and he rarely talked. Then one day I was passing his desk and happened to notice a fly-tying manual under his chair. I picked it up.

"Do you tie flies?" I asked.

His eyes lit up. "Yeah. Do you?"

"All the time!"

Suddenly we had something in common. And our

relationship changed. We swapped a few of our favorite fly patterns and shared fishing stories. More important, we broke the ice. He started asking questions in class. And as he understood his assignments better, his test scores went up. He went from being an average student to an excellent student. As his relationship with his teacher improved, so did his performance.

The same thing can happen to you.

Keep in mind that most teachers enjoy young people. They enjoy getting to know their students. So let them. Make it a point to visit for a moment before or after class once in a while. If you get to school early one day, or if you have to stay late, drop in on one of them to say hi.

The better your teachers know you, the better they'll be able to teach you. And the better your relationship is, the more likely you'll be able to prevent problems from ever happening.

It also helps to *be sure that you're part of the class.*

Being part of the class means more than just being in the room every day. It means taking part and being involved. So go out of your way to participate. If your teacher asks a question, be brave enough to raise your hand, even if you're not sure of the answer. Involve yourself in group discussions and activities.

By doing this, you'll accomplish two things. You'll be setting yourself apart from the students who keep their noses glued to their desks, and you'll be proving that you're interested in what's going on. Both things impress teachers.

Another hint is to *keep all of your old tests, papers, and assignments.*

There are a couple of reasons for this. For one thing, they make excellent study guides for when you need to review something.

More important, they're helpful if you ever disagree with a teacher over a grade. Remember that your teachers have to keep track of a lot of students. Mistakes are easy to make. But if you keep all of your work, you'll have a complete record of your progress.

Finally, remember to *use common sense.*

Right from the very first day of class, go out of your way to prove that you're serious about your work. Follow these five tips:

First, *be on time to class.* And this doesn't mean bursting inside the room just as the bell rings. Being late to class not only shows your lack of interest in the class but it's also disrespectful to your teacher.

Second, *be prepared.* Make sure you've got all the books, papers, pencils, and other supplies you need before class starts. Most good teachers like to start class right away. And students who need to go around the room borrowing paper and pencils distract not only the teacher but everyone else in the room, too.

Third, *spend your class time working.* If you put your best effort into your work, most teachers will notice. And they'll appreciate it. On the other hand, if you spend your time writing notes or, even worse, doing work from another class, you're telling your teacher that *his* class is not important to you.

Fourth, *be reliable.* Who knows? Maybe your dog *did* eat your homework. But your teachers know every excuse in the book, and they're tired of hearing them. But if you set a pattern of being reliable, of being on time with every assignment, your teachers will be more willing to understand when emergencies do occur.

Finally, *think!* There are two no-no's when dealing with teachers. For instance, you never, *ever* say things like, "I'm not going to be here tomorrow . . . are we going to do anything important?" (Teachers like to believe that *everything* they do is important.)

And never say, "I didn't have time to finish my assignment last night . . . I had to get my English done." In both cases you're telling your teacher that his class is low on your priority list.

No matter how well you follow these tips, you'll occasionally run into teachers who don't respond. After all, teachers are human like everyone else. Some are probably in the wrong profession. And no matter what you do, some are just plain hard to get along with.

When you wind up with a difficult teacher, your first reaction might be to transfer out of the class. But that's usually not the best solution. After all, you're going to run into difficult people all your life. You'll deal with them in school, on your mission, in your career, even at church. Most of the time you can't solve the problem by running away. So you might as well learn how to make the best of it.

If things become intolerable, discuss it with your parents. Visit the school counselor. Talk it over with another teacher or even the principal if you have to. Transferring *might* be the only answer. But leave it as a last resort. I firmly believe that learning to get along with an unpleasant teacher is one of the most valuable lessons you can ever learn.

And remember that just because you have problems with a teacher doesn't necessarily mean that he's a bad person.

When I was in college I once had a disagreement with one of my professors. We went into his office and shouted at one another for nearly half an hour. Later, as I thought about it, I was embarrassed that I had made such a scene. But I still believed I was right just as firmly as he believed I was wrong.

The worst part, though, came the first day of the next semester. I had to change my class schedule at the last minute, and as luck would have it, I needed to take a certain newswriting class. Mr. Thomas was the only professor teaching it. To make things even worse, I had to ask him personally for permission to be in his class.

I fully expected him to say no. He had every reason to. Especially after the mean things I had said to him.

But he signed my transfer slip without a word. And then throughout the semester he treated me as well as any other student. He didn't hold a grudge, and he never acted as if anything had ever happened between us.

It wasn't an easy situation for either of us. And I respected him for being so professional about it.

Many of the teachers you deal with will be the same. You may not agree on certain things. You might argue or even shout at one another. But remember that chances are the teacher is still a good person. So if you manage to work things out, let bygones be bygones. Don't hold anything against him. And if you do end up transferring, don't go around badmouthing him to your friends. You're out of his class, so leave it at that.

Because school is such a big part of your life, here's a final piece of advice. Go out of your way to become special friends with at least one teacher every year.

There are many reasons for this. A teacher not only has a great deal to offer in the way of knowledge, but you spend a lot of time at school and you never know when having a friend on the inside might help. You might need access to a phone, for instance. Or a copy machine. Maybe you're having a bad day and you just need someone to talk to.

I once had a student named Michelle in my ninth-grade geometry class. She was the most lively, energetic student I had. So when she spent half the period with her eyes closed and her head bent over her desk one day, I asked her to step into the hall for a talk.

"Are you okay?" I asked.

She looked at me blankly. "Yeah. I had to have two teeth pulled this morning. And the shots are starting to wear off."

I winced. "Ouch. You gonna be all right?"

She nodded. "Yeah. I'll be okay."

An hour later, though, I was just finishing up the lesson in my next class when Michelle appeared in the doorway. She was waving frantically.

"Just a moment," I told my class. "I'll be right back."

I walked into the hall, where Michelle was trembling like a leaf. Her face was pale and tears rolled down her cheeks.

"What's the matter?"

"The shots wore off," she said, bouncing up and down in an effort to relieve the pain. "And I hurt! I hurt so bad I can't stand it!"

"Didn't the dentist give you any painkillers?" I asked.

"Yes! But my dad doesn't want me to take them. I tried to call him, but he's not at work. And I can't find my mom!"

"Okay, okay," I said. "What do you want me to do?"

The tears rushed down her face. "I hurt so bad I can't think. I need somebody to tell me what to do!"

Michelle was in so much pain that I hurt just watching her. And I hated seeing her in such agony. But I knew what to do. I knew one of Michelle's uncles. We called him and he took her straight back to the dentist.

Most people become teachers because they like people . . . especially young people. So when you have a problem, they're usually good people to turn to.

Make sure you always know one teacher you can go to if you have a problem or need help in a crisis.

Teachers can have a wonderful impact on your life if you'll let them. Take the time to develop good, working relationships with them. Get to know them, and let them get to know you, too. Become part of their class and take advantage of the opportunities they present to you.

When you have good relationships with your teachers you'll learn more, you'll be more confident, and you'll be more successful in school. And you'll have a lot more fun, too!

Tips to Remember

- Be friendly with all your teachers—even the ornery ones. (They probably need it the most!) Say hi when you pass them in the hall or enter their room. Be brave enough to poke your head in the door once in a while just to say hi.

- Make sure your teachers know you as a person. Find ways to let them know about your talents, interests, and hobbies. The more a teacher understands you, the better she'll be able to teach you. (And the easier it will be for her to tolerate your imperfections.)

- Become part of every class you're in. Don't be afraid to sit on the front row. Participate in class discussions. Ask questions. Volunteer answers.

- Try—really *try*—to work out problems when you have them. If your teacher seems unwilling to cooperate, discuss the situation with your parents, a counselor, or the principal. Don't transfer except as a *last* resort.

- Get in the habit of keeping old tests and assignments. Then, if you ever have a disagreement over a grade, you'll have a written record of your progress.

- Become special friends with at least one teacher every year. Not only will you bless their lives, but they'll bless yours, too. And you never know when you might need their help in a crisis.

11

THE BATTLE OF
MAPLE DELL

Dealing with Employers

Cordell Mulcady was paddling frantically with both hands. When he looked up, his eyes were wide with panic.

"Shane, look out! Behind us!"

I turned as a canoe loaded with Boy Scouts sliced through the water towards us. We tried to turn, but before we could paddle away a dozen hands grabbed our canoe and tried to tip it. Cold lake water poured in over the sides. Cordell and I tried to keep our balance, but it was no use. We were outnumbered.

"Abandon ship!" Cordell yelled. "Abandon ship!"

I didn't have to be told twice. I jumped out of the canoe and into the lake an instant before it flipped.

Cordy flailed at the water.

"Ah . . . ah . . . ah! This is *so* cold!"

I was freezing too, but I wasn't going down without taking somebody with me. Ducking my head I stroked for the canoe that swamped us. The Scouts saw me coming and tried to get away, but it was too late. I grabbed their canoe, put my weight on the side, then suddenly let go. The canoe flipped neatly, spilling its crew into the lake.

"All right!" Cordell shouted. "Way to go!"

Treading water, I gave Cordell a high five, then looked around the lake. Chaos was everywhere. Boys wearing orange life jackets bobbed around canoes half-filled with water. There wasn't a dry boat afloat anywhere.

It was the worst naval disaster since Pearl Harbor.

And I was being paid to be part of it.

I was spending the summer working at Boy Scout camp. Every Friday we staged what we called the Battle of Maple Dell. Cramming every canoe in camp full of as many boys as we could, we floated into the middle of the lake. When the camp director blew his whistle, everyone began swamping everyone else. The last boat afloat was the winner.

There was only one rule. As soon as your boat was swamped you were out of the game and were supposed to swim politely back to shore.

Ha!

What actually happened was that as soon as someone swamped you, you got even by sinking them back, and then you both ganged up to sink someone else. One week the camp director tried to prevent this by sending out a couple of rowboats filled with referees. They were supposed to send people back to shore as soon as they got swamped. But it didn't work. Two minutes after the battle started, a dozen canoes attacked the rowboats. The referees were the first ones into the lake.

I loved working at Scout camp. During the day I taught classes at the rifle range. In the afternoon I went hiking, swimming, and boating. At night I played games or told stories around troop campfires. It was the best job I ever had.

It was so much fun, in fact, that I went back year after year. I eventually became program director of the Beaver High Adventure Base and the Scofield Aquatics Base.

Chances are, you have a summer or after-school job too. It may not be as exciting as working at Scout camp, but that's okay. Part-time jobs are a great way of earning spending money. Besides that, a good job teaches you responsibility and good work habits. And it's a great way to make new friends.

When I was in high school I worked part-time at an ice-cream store in the local mall. The friends I made there were the best I had. We had a terrific boss who treated us like adults. He trusted us and gave us plenty of responsibility and independence.

Not everyone is so lucky. Unlike school teachers (who usually like kids), many employers are not skilled at working with young people. Many of them hire high school and college students simply because they have to. Many of them have never been trained to work with teenagers.

A young woman I know named Nancy found a summer job working as a clerk for the county recorder. It was the first real job she had ever had. But even though she was inexperienced, she was determined to do her best.

The only problem was that her supervisor had never worked with a teenager before. From the very first day she expected Nancy to be as skilled as the older, more experienced employees. She actually complained that Nancy asked too many questions.

Well, not *every* employer you have is going to be perfect. And it's for those times that this chapter will help you.

As with so many other situations, when you're trying to survive your experience with an employer the best defense is a good offense. From the first day you start working, be the best employee you can be. Not only is that the right thing to do—whether you're a cook, a busboy, a custodian, or a secretary—but also it will teach you good work habits. Then, as you begin finding better and better jobs, you'll already have the good work habits you need in order to succeed.

Keep these tips in mind:

First, *be on time.* Show up early enough that you don't have to waste "work" time changing clothes or getting ready.

Second, *be teachable.* If your boss wants you to sweep the floor a certain way, do it. Most employers have reasons for doing things the way they do. And many of them have been in business long enough to know the quickest, most effective ways of doing things. So listen to what they want you to do, then do your best at it.

I know a man who owns several fast-food franchises. Over the years he's hired hundreds of teenagers. "I love working with young people," he said. "The only time I have trouble is when they come to work with a Burger King attitude."

"A Burger King attitude?"

"Yes. That's where they want to do everything *their* way."

Remember that it's your employer's store. *Her* way is the way that counts.

This doesn't mean that you might not have a better idea once in a while; but when you do, wait for the right moment to bring it up. Then leave the final decision to your boss. If she doesn't like it, well, she *is* the boss. She can ask you to do things any way she wants.

Third, *be honest.* And I'm not talking about stealing. (Hopefully that's something we don't need to talk about!) If you make a mistake and your boss questions you about it, don't fudge or make excuses. Instead, admit your mistake. Apologize and promise to do better.

Better yet, if you make a mistake and realize it, tell your boss before he finds out about it. Then, if possible, do everything you can to make things right.

I remember defrosting the freezers one Saturday night when I was working at the ice-cream store. I turned off the freezers, removed all the ice cream, sponged off the frost, and replaced the ice cream.

But I forgot to turn the freezers back on.

It wasn't until late the next afternoon that it hit me. I almost died. I dashed back to the store to find almost sixty gallons of melted ice cream running in the freezers.

After I had cleaned everything up, I gathered up my courage and called my boss. I had to tell him that I had just ruined more than two hundred dollars' worth of ice cream.

Well, he took the news a lot better than I thought he would. He didn't fire me (could you have blamed him?), and he didn't even make me pay for the ice cream (which I was expecting I would have to do). But what really surprised me was that the next time the freezers needed defrosting he scheduled *me* to do it. I guess he knew that I'd learned my lesson, and I had! Not only did I remember to turn the freezers back on this time, but I went back *three* times over the weekend to make sure.

Fourth, *be happy.* Learn to find the fun in your work.

While I was at Scout camp I once had a thirteen-year-old assistant named Bryan. At the end of the

week we were going from campsite to campsite, helping troops as they broke camp and prepared to leave.
When we found one troop struggling to break camp,
we decided to help out by taking a bottle of Pine-Sol
and cleaning out their latrine for them.

I love Pine-Sol (it smells so good), so I was using
plenty. I poured about half a bottle over the wooden
toilet, then accidentally dropped the lid, splashing
Pine-Sol all over the place. At that moment I happened
to be telling a joke (I can be fun to work with when I
want to be) and Bryan was laughing with his mouth
open.

You've probably already guessed what happened.
And you're right. He got a whole mouthful.

As we went from campsite to campsite, I told the
adventure over and over again. After a while, though, I
turned to Bryan. "I hope you don't mind me telling
that story," I said. "I hope it doesn't embarrass you."

He just laughed. "No, it's okay," he assured me.
"You always make *me* sound like the hero."

I loved Bryan for that. He had such a good attitude
that when he was around, even such ugly work as
scrubbing outhouses became fun.

You can be the same way. No matter what your job
is, you can go to work every day with a smile on your
face and make the job more fun for everyone. If you attack your job with a good attitude, the quality of your
work will improve. Your co-workers will work better,
too. The time will fly. And your employer will notice.

Fifth, *finish what you start.* If you get off at five but
you haven't finished sweeping the floor, don't just
drop the broom and take off. Finish the job, even if
you don't get paid for the extra time.

I once spent a day watching a crew of teenagers
who were spending the summer working for the Forest
Service. They were building a fence around a camp-

ground when it started to rain. As quick as they could, everyone ran for cover. They were huddling beneath a pine tree when someone pointed.

"What in the world are those guys doing?"

Everyone looked. Tom and Eric, the two youngest boys on the crew, were standing out in the rain still working on the fence. A lot of the older boys laughed, but Tom and Eric were just finishing the job they were assigned to do. And one person who *wasn't* laughing was the camp ranger. Once a week he took the outstanding crew members of the week to town for a steak dinner and a movie. Tom and Eric both shared the honor that week.

The world is full of people who start things, but it needs more people who are willing to finish what they start. Show your boss that you have the integrity and character to complete the jobs you're given.

Sixth, *be willing to go the extra mile.*

I talked with one employer who complained that his employees never did a thing more than they were asked to do. Not a thing.

One time, he said, he placed several large boxes in a hallway, stacking them so that people had to go out of their way to get past them. Beneath one of them he placed a five-dollar bill with a note that read: "Thank you for moving these boxes. Please keep this bill as a token of my appreciation."

"And you know what?" he asked. "Those boxes stayed there *all* day. Not one person bothered to move them or even ask if they were there for a reason."

If you want to make points with your boss, keep this single tip in mind: a good employee is one who makes his boss's job easier.

When I was at summer camp, I was once asked to teach a rifle class at six o'clock the next morning.

"You don't need to be there, though," I told my

three assistants. "It was my own fault for scheduling something that early, and you guys don't need to suffer for my mistakes."

When I walked onto the rifle range at six the next morning, though, Bryan (of Pine-Sol fame) was already there setting out rifles. Little things like that made Bryan the best assistant I ever had.

When I was going to college I worked part-time as a sportswriter (now *there* was a fun job!). I enjoyed the work, and I spent as much time covering ball games as I spent in classes.

One day I walked into the office to find my boss boiling mad.

"What's the matter?"

"Plenty," she told me. "There's a problem with the basketball brochures. I have to spend all day tomorrow with the printer, and now there's no one to cover the golf tournament."

Almost without thinking I said, "I'll do it."

She looked at me skeptically. I was new on the job and golf wasn't part of my beat. "Do you know anything about golf?"

"No. But I'm willing to learn."

She hesitated another moment, then gave me a crash course in golf writing. I spent the rest of the day reading golf stories, trying to get a feel for them. I covered the tournament for the next three days and had so much fun that I asked to have golf added to my regular assignments.

I wasn't just trying to score points when I did this. I was just trying to help out. And it turned out to be one of the highlights of my career.

Go out of your way to help. If you see a spill in the hallway, take a minute to clean it up. If you see something that needs to be done, don't wait to be asked. Just do it!

Seventh, *ask for help when you need it.* This is hard to do sometimes. Many teenagers hate to ask questions, thinking they'll appear dumb or worrying that they'll be bothering the boss.

But ask anyway. It's a thousand times better to risk a moment of embarrassment than to make a costly mistake.

Eighth, *be dependable.* Prove to your boss that she can leave you to do a job and know it will get done right.

When you begin any new job, it's reasonable for an employer to watch you closely. But after a while she should be leaving you alone more and more.

The important thing is that when she learns she can count on you, she becomes free to do other things. Remember that you are there to make her job easier. So don't make her worry about you. Prove that she can leave you alone, knowing that you'll get the job done right.

Despite these tips, it's possible (even likely) that someday you'll have an employer who doesn't respond. No matter what you do, he'll manage to make your life miserable.

If this happens to you, there are a couple of things you can do. First, try talking to him about it. Let him know how you feel. If you don't feel comfortable doing this, talk it over with *his* supervisor or another, older employee. Share your concerns with your parents, too. They might have additional suggestions.

If after a while things don't improve, you have two choices. If you like the job and want to keep it, you can accept the fact that you've done your best to make peace. Then let it go at that.

Or you can find another job.

Earning money is just one of the benefits of having a part-time job. The experience you gain handling responsibility and working with other people will help you for the rest of your life.

So don't be like so many people who have to force themselves to work each day. No matter what your job is, dive into it with a good attitude and a smile on your face. Do the best job you can.

Make the most of it!

Tips to Remember

- When you go to work, do the best job you can. Show up on time and don't quit early. Dress appropriately for the work you do.

- Be teachable. Learn how your employer wants things done, then do them her way. If you believe you have a better idea, present it at an appropriate time.

- Be honest. Everyone slips up once in a while, so admit your mistakes when you make them. Learn from the experience and don't make the same mistake twice.

- Be happy! Go to work with a good attitude and make the job more fun for everyone around you. Share your smile with your employer, co-workers, and customers.

- Be a self-starter. Don't wait to be given things to do. Look for things that need to be done and do them. Finish the jobs you start. Go the extra mile.

- Ask for help when you need it. It's far better to risk a moment of embarrassment than to make a costly mistake. Besides, most employers will appreciate the fact that you're trying to do things right.

12

THEY DIDN'T HAVE DENTISTS IN THE BOOK OF MORMON!

Working with Church Leaders

"You want me to do what?"

The bishop looked over at her with his most serious expression. "We need you in the Young Women's program," he said. "I'm calling you to be president of the Laurel class."

Karen Ericksen sat stunned in her chair. She had just had her seventeenth birthday, and she had expected this to be a standard how-are-you-and-is-there-anything-I-can-do-for-you interview. She was totally unprepared for the bishop's bombshell.

"You're a wonderful young woman," Bishop Chase continued. "You have talents and abilities that will bless the program. Will you accept?"

Karen nodded weakly. "Yes."

"Good!" The bishop beamed, shaking her hand

warmly. "Sister Garrison will be contacting you. She's the class adviser. She's looking forward to working with you."

Karen walked home, still not quite believing what had happened. You see, Karen's family was not very active in the Church. Karen attended most of her meetings anyway, but after she had had an unpleasant experience with an adviser she had stopped going to Young Women.

Now she was being called to be class president. She not only accepted, but she did a wonderful job. She worked well with her new adviser and together they filled the Laurel program with fun, energy, and love.

"Working with Sister Garrison is the best thing that ever happened to me," Karen said. "I never knew I had a testimony until I began working with her."

When the bishop asked Karen and Sister Garrison to work together, he did two things. He changed Karen's life. And he created a successful Laurel class.

One thing that sets Church leaders apart from other adults is that they're called by your Heavenly Father to work with you. You have to remember that whether you get along with them or not, the Lord *wants* you together. That's why it's so important that you do your best to get along with them.

Besides, Church leaders are among the finest adults you will ever work with. The help they can give you cannot be measured in earthly terms.

I remember having a Sunday School teacher named Brad who gave me a new appreciation for reading the scriptures. It started because he could rattle off stories from the scriptures at the drop of a hat. We used to tease him about it. Then we made a game of it. We'd think up a word, and he would have to tell us a story from the scriptures that related to it.

"Sluffing," we said once.

"Enos used to sluff church and go hunting," Brad said without a moment's hesitation. "He sluffed so often that he started to feel bad about it. So he began to pray, and before he knew it, he'd been on his knees all day and night . . ."

(I later looked up the story of Enos and it didn't say a word about sluffing church. When I asked Brad about it he was unfazed. He just said, "Where does it say that he didn't?")

Another time we said, "Dating."

"That's a good one," Brad replied. "Remember Laman and Lemuel? All they ever did was complain. When Lehi sent them back to Jerusalem they moaned and groaned the whole way. Then he sent them back to get wives." Brad laughed. "And that was the *only* time they didn't complain about it!"

One time, not realizing that Brad was eavesdropping, my friend Cannon was talking about going to the dentist.

"I don't think they had dentists in the Book of Mormon," Brad said, as if he were part of the conversation all along. "But it does say that Ether used to dwell in a cavity."

Hoo boy!

All of this may seem silly. But Brad got us excited about reading the scriptures. After hearing a few of his stories we'd dash home to read the scriptural accounts for ourselves. Sometimes we'd be checking to make certain that he'd told them correctly. But more often we were just anxious to find out more.

I remember another Church leader who had a good influence on me. He was a member of our bishopric and he once went on a Scout camp-out with us. After dinner Brother Andrews and I went for a hike in the woods. As we hiked, we talked. He told me about being called to be in the bishopric, and he shared a few of his experiences.

I remember feeling good as I talked with him. And I believe that on that hike I felt the first stirrings of my own testimony.

For the most part, Church leaders are kind, sensitive individuals. It doesn't seem possible that you would ever have problems with them. But it happens.

I once talked with a young man named Duke. A bright, energetic twelve-year-old, he was so sensitive to the needs and feelings of other people that I couldn't picture anyone not liking him.

"But my Scoutmaster sure hates me," he insisted.

I couldn't believe it. "Your Scoutmaster? You're kidding."

"I'm not. At Scout camp he threw me down and almost wouldn't let me have dinner."

That didn't sound like any Scoutmaster I'd ever known, so I asked to hear the whole story. Duke said the problems all started when the troop campsite got messy.

"All right," Mr. Harris said one night before dinner. "I want everyone to go out and pick up thirty pieces of litter. We'll eat as soon as everyone's finished."

The boys were barbecuing pork chops that night, and Duke wanted to be first in line. He dashed off to a spot near his tent, picked up thirty pieces of litter, and hurried to get back in line. He was so fast that Mr. Harris didn't believe he'd done his share.

"Duke!" he shouted. "Get *out* of the line and don't come back until you've picked up thirty pieces of trash!"

"But I did!" Duke protested.

"Make it *sixty* pieces," Harris ordered. (He didn't like boys talking back to him.)

"But I've already done my share!"

"A hundred pieces . . . and you can wash everyone's dishes tonight."

"But—"

Harris had had enough. He pulled Duke out of line so hard that he fell down. "Now go," he said. "And don't come back until you're done."

So Duke trudged through the campsite picking up litter. By now things were pretty well cleaned up, and finding a hundred pieces wasn't easy. By the time he was done, all the best pork chops were gone, and the ones that were still left were cold.

"And it wasn't even my fault," Duke insisted. "Mr. Harris wouldn't even listen to me. He's just so stubborn."

The worst part was that Mr. Harris was also *Brother* Harris. Besides being Scoutmaster, he was also the deacons quorum adviser. And he didn't treat Duke any better in priesthood meetings than he had at camp.

"He hasn't liked me ever since camp," Duke said. "Once I gave a talk in opening exercises, and he never even said anything about it. Sometimes I pass him in the hall and he won't even look at me."

Well, everyone's human. Even members of the Church. But because it's church, you need to be extra sensitive as you work with others. To enjoy the Lord's help, inspiration, and blessings, you have to avoid contention and bad feelings.

A couple of years ago I attended a youth conference in South Dakota. A committee made up almost entirely of teenagers planned the two-day conference down to the last details. Except for one thing: the conference was to include a dance, and the adult supervisor insisted on personally approving every song that was to be played.

That was okay, except for the fact that Brother Marshall didn't seem to have any reason for rejecting some of the records the committee had selected. "We didn't pick any bad songs to begin with," said Rick, who was the youth chairman of the dance committee. "He made us feel like he was rejecting songs just because he didn't like them."

It happened that Rick's father was serving as stake president at the time and could have solved the problem. But he refused to get involved. "It's Brother Marshall's decision," he told Rick. "Work things out with him."

So the committee talked things over and finally reached a compromise. They sat down with Brother Marshall to discuss what was happening. They listed each of the songs he had rejected and explained why they thought they were appropriate. Brother Marshall then listened to each song again. He still rejected some of them. But he changed his mind about others.

The point is that many of the problems you have with Church leaders can be solved by simply sitting down and talking things over with them.

And keep in mind that most of the leaders you work with will be called *advisers.* That means they are not supposed to make all the decisions. In fact, their role is to guide and direct you as *you* make the decisions.

Now, if you want *your* program to run that way, prove that you can handle it. Show that you can take charge. Prove that you're responsible enough to deserve it.

One of the reasons why so many adults take over the youth programs is that most young people don't handle them properly themselves. Some teenagers are afraid to. Others don't realize that they're supposed to.

But if you want to be in charge, take charge. If you are a class or quorum president, it is *your* job to preside over and conduct your weekly meetings. So do it! Start the meeting on time. Get everyone quiet. Consult with your advisers beforehand and let them know exactly what they can do to help.

Remember that because they're adults, many leaders will automatically expect to be in charge. You'll have to handle them carefully. Let them know that they're welcome, needed, and important to the program. Listen to what they have to say and show them that their counsel is appreciated. But let them see by your actions that *you* are in charge of the program.

No matter how well you work with your advisers, there will be times when you have disagreements. When this happens, the most important thing is to avoid arguing. Contention has no place in the Church. If you can't solve the problem through discussion, consult with the bishop. (It's best if you approach the bishop together, then your advisers won't feel that you are going behind their backs. Remember that if you are going to work together successfully, you must have a good relationship.)

Another key is to hold regular presidency meetings. This will do four things. It will ensure that you are prepared for your next class and for any activities you have coming up. It will give you a chance to determine how to help individual members of your class. It will give your advisers a chance to offer suggestions. And it will show your leaders that you are serious about your position.

Finally, be wise enough to listen when your advisers counsel you. After all, the Lord called them to assist you, so it's fair to believe they have something important to offer.

A young woman named Rachelle told me about a comment that her Laurel adviser once made in presidency meeting. "We need to be aware of Ericka," Sister

Jensen said. "I think she's having trouble adjusting since she moved here."

Ericka was new in the ward. She didn't have many friends yet in school, and she was beginning to drift toward the wrong crowds. Many of the Laurels hesitated making friends with her for that very reason.

"When you're lonely, sometimes any friend is welcome," Sister Jensen said. "Maybe Ericka associates with those other girls because they're the only ones who pay any attention to her."

"I'd never thought of it that way," Rachelle told me. "And I never forgot it. We started including Ericka in the things we did and it made a world of difference to her."

Again, remember that the Lord gave you your adviser for a reason. So trust his judgment. Form good, working relationships with your Church leaders.

The rewards will bless you not only now but also through all eternity.

Tips to Remember

- Always remember that your Church leaders have been called by your Heavenly Father. Have faith that *he* wants them working with you. So get close to them. Listen to their counsel.

- If you do have a disagreement with a Church leader, go out of your way to avoid arguing and any form of contention. This is good advice when working with any adult, but it's doubly important here. If you allow bad feelings to sour your relationships, you'll miss out on the Lord's help and blessings.

- If you can't work out a disagreement peacefully, ask the bishop for help. Remember to approach him together with your adviser.

- When you are called to lead a class or quorum, *do it!* Take charge. Develop and practice your leadership skills. Hold regular presidency meetings. Work closely with your advisers to bless the lives of the youth in your program.

13

RANTING, RAVING, AND BLOWING YOUR COOL

When You Feel Like Going to Battle

You stole my story!"

John Price, the faculty adviser to BYU's student newspaper, compared the stories I'd slapped down on his desk and shook his head. His voice was as calm as milk.

"Well, it appears that we might have made a mistake. But we didn't steal your story."

I felt the temperature in the room go up ten degrees. "How can you say that? Look right there! That's *my* story! With somebody else's name on it!"

He remained unruffled. "It's a simple mistake. That's all."

I couldn't believe it. I had just written a story on BYU's newest athlete, a runner from Ireland who was one of the best women marathoners in the world. It

was my first feature story for BYU's Sports Informa-
tion Office, and I had spent hours working on it.

Finally, after I had it polished to perfection, I sub-
mitted it to all of the papers that covered BYU sports,
including BYU's *Daily Universe.*

Two days later the *Universe* ran it . . . with another
writer's name attached. Oh, a few paragraphs had
been switched around here and there. But they were
still word for word the way I had written them.

It was plagiarism, clear and simple.

And I was hopping mad.

But the most frustrating thing was that Mr. Price
didn't seem to think it was a big deal. While I ranted
and raved, he sat smugly at his desk with a half-smile
on his face.

And that only made things worse.

I didn't intend to blow up at him, but the more he
tried to brush me off, the madder I got. My friend Tami
was with me, and when I finally stormed away she
took me by the arm.

"Are you okay?"

I took a deep breath and checked my pulse. It was
still racing. "Yeah," I said. "I'm okay."

"I've never seen you like that before," she said.
"You scared me."

And that embarrassed me. Tami was a good friend
of mine, and I was ashamed that she had seen me act-
ing the way I had.

Besides that, I knew I was wrong. Regardless of
what the paper had done with my story, there were
better ways of handling the situation. I could have let
my boss take care of it, for instance. Or maybe I could
have written a complaint to the department chairman.

The one thing I shouldn't have done was go
screaming into Price's office the way I had.

Besides making a fool of myself, I was afraid I was

going to lose my job. I spent the next week tiptoeing in and out of the office, worrying that each day would be my last.

As it turned out, I didn't get fired. I didn't even get a reprimand. But I felt so bad that I didn't need one. I knew I had goofed up, and I kicked myself again and again for it.

I have a friend named Carleen who had a similar experience. She played first-chair saxophone in her high school's stage band. One day, when the second-chair player challenged her, the band director switched them. "Carleen actually played the piece better," the teacher admitted. "But I think Mike was trying harder."

Carleen looked up. "Excuse me? You think he was *trying* harder? Since when does that matter?"

"Since today. Now switch places."

"I'm not switching. You *said* I played better. How hard I have to try has nothing to do with it."

"Carleen, I don't want a scene here. Let's discuss it later."

Carleen did go in to talk about it later. But things just went from bad to worse. She believed she had been treated unfairly, but her teacher wasn't going to change his mind. Carleen was so mad, in fact, that she stormed out of his office and never went back.

The sad thing is that this is a case where everyone lost. Carleen missed out on playing with the band for the rest of the year. And the band lost a talented musician.

As you're growing up, there will be times when you might feel like squaring off against an adult, too. A teacher might unfairly give you a bad grade. An employer might suspend, fine, or even fire you. Your parents might not allow you to attend a big dance. A neighbor might complain about the noise you make.

When it happens, you might feel like screaming and

shouting. But that won't solve the problem. And in most cases it will only make things worse.

You might have a shouting match with your teacher, for instance, but then you have to go back to his class the next day. You may have an argument with your neighbor, but since you live so close you're still going to see him every day for years to come.

So you need to learn to handle things maturely.

Being able to work your way out of sticky confrontations is a valuable survival skill. And once you learn to do it without blowing your top, you'll find many problems easier to deal with. So let's look at a couple of ways of doing that.

First, when you have a problem with an adult, *choose the right time and place to work it out.*

If you're trying to avoid a nasty scene, you don't want to approach someone when they're already under a lot of stress. That's why you never want to try working out a problem with a teacher just before class. Not only is there not enough time for a serious discussion, but she's probably got enough on her mind as it is.

And you never want to try working out difficulties with your parents when they're busy paying bills, changing diapers, or struggling with the plumbing. At times like these, they're probably not in the best of moods anyway. And confronting them with another problem will just make things worse.

So choose a time to talk when they're likely to be calm and relaxed. Make sure they'll be able to concentrate on your discussion.

Second, *stay calm.*

This can be tough, especially if you've been wronged and your blood pressure is already past the boiling point. But getting into a shouting match will only make things worse.

I have a seventeen-year-old friend named Scott who once bought a new battery for his car. But a week later he found that all the battery fluid had leaked out. Digging up his receipt, he hauled the battery back to the store. "I bought this a week ago," he told the clerk. "And it's already dead. It's got a leak somewhere."

The clerk examined the battery for a moment, then pried open the caps on top. "Well, here's your problem," he said. "The battery fluid's all gone."

"I know," Scott said. "It has a leak."

"See, you have to keep the cells filled. Otherwise, the battery loses its charge and the plates rust."

"I know that. But it leaks."

"I'm sure it's a good battery. But you can't expect us to replace it if you don't take care of it."

"I know that. But it leaks."

"See, look right in here . . . the plates are already starting to rust."

By then, Scott felt ready to explode. But rather than blow up, he just asked to talk with the store manager.

"He's not going to be able to help you any more than I can," the clerk said. "No battery is going to work if you don't keep it filled."

Scott was trying hard not to scream. But finally the manager came out and peered into the battery. He looked as if he, too, was about to chastise Scott for not keeping it filled when he noticed a spot of moisture on the counter. He studied it for a moment, then made a startling announcement. "Well, here's the problem . . . it's leaking."

It was all Scott could do not to punch somebody. "The whole thing would have been kind of funny," he told me, "if it just hadn't been so *frustrating!*"

If a talk with an adult begins deteriorating to the point that you *do* start shouting, the best thing you can do is walk away. Wait until everyone has cooled down, and then either try it again or try talking to somebody else. (If your problem is with a teacher, for instance, try talking to the principal or a counselor. If it's with your boss, try talking to *her* supervisor. If it's with one of your parents, try discussing it with your other parent.)

Whatever the situation, the minute you lose your temper you lose any hope of solving the problem.

So bite your tongue. Clench your fists. Close your eyes and count to a thousand if you have to. But *stay calm!*

Third, *don't attack the person you're talking to.*

When somebody wrongs you, it's normal to feel angry. And it's easy to say mean things. But when you attack someone, he'll become defensive. He'll concentrate on defending himself rather than on solving the problem.

So be careful how you phrase things. If you suspect that your employer has made a mistake on your paycheck, don't barge into her office saying, "Hey, you ripped me off!" Instead, show her copies of your check and time card and say, "There's something I don't understand about my paycheck this week. I was wondering if you would help me figure it out."

If you do this, the other person won't feel threatened. He'll be able to concentrate on the problem. Besides that, if it ever turns out that the mistake is *your* fault, you're going to feel pretty silly if you went in causing a fuss.

I bought a basketball not too long ago, and when I got home I noticed that I'd been charged twice for it. So I took the receipt back to the store. "There's a problem," I said. "I bought a basketball here a little while ago, and I think I was overcharged for it."

The clerk examined the receipt. And sure enough,

the price of the basketball was listed twice. But she noticed something that I hadn't. After the second charge were the words *voided item.*

In other words, the clerk had entered the price of the ball twice, had realized her mistake, and then had voided the second entry.

I felt pretty silly for not having noticed it myself. But it was not nearly as bad as if I had gone in shouting, "Hey, you ripped me off, you morons!"

Fourth, *listen to the other person's point of view.*

There will be times when neither of you is actually wrong. When that happens, it's important that you keep an open mind. Make sure you don't blame the wrong person for the mistake.

I have a friend named Jan who received a C- one term in her French class. "But I had earned an A," she told me. "I *knew* I had earned an A. It was my best class. I had A's on all my tests and I got good grades on all of my assignments."

When Mr. Turner checked his score book, though, things weren't as rosy as Jan claimed. According to his records, Jan had a 67 percent on one test and she had completely missed another one.

Jan knew that wasn't right. So that night she went digging through all her old papers and found the two tests in question. She had A's on both of them. She showed them to Mr. Turner, who double-checked his records.

And then he figured out what was wrong. He was using a new grading program, and the computer had switched Jan's scores with another student who had the same last name. It was an innocent mistake. And it wasn't anyone's fault.

Many of the problems you have with adults will be the same way. So keep an open mind and don't blame people for something that might not be their fault.

Misunderstandings are unfortunate, but they happen. So the next time you feel like squaring off against an adult, remember to be patient. Wait for the right time to work things out, then stay calm. Don't attack the person you're talking with, and listen to his or her point of view.

Learning to work out your problems will set you apart, not only as a teenager but as an adult, too.

Tips to Remember

- Don't be afraid to stick up for yourself. Don't go looking for trouble, but if you feel that an adult has wronged you somehow, don't be afraid to correct the situation.

- Think before you act. Don't try confronting an adult when you're all worked up. Instead, wait for the right time and place.

- No matter what happens, stay calm. If the discussion starts turning ugly, walk away. Wait until everyone has calmed down, and then try again.

- Try to keep the discussion from becoming personal. Don't attack the person you're talking to and don't make accusations. If you do this, he won't become defensive. He'll be able to concentrate on the problem without feeling threatened.

- Listen to the other person's point of view. Sometimes things happen that aren't anyone's fault. Don't get upset with someone for something that might be an innocent mistake.

14

CLIMBING IN THE ROCKS

Final Thoughts

On belay!"

I checked my ropes one final time and braced my feet against the rock. "Belay is on!"

"Climbing!"

"Climb on!"

I began taking up slack as my friend Rick, who was seventy-five feet below me, began scaling the sheer wall of the red cliff. He moved quickly at first, then slowed as the cracks and bumps that gave him toe and finger holds became fewer and farther between. Then he stopped.

"Tension!"

I quickly locked up the rope. "Tension!" I held on tight as Rick tried to scramble around a sharp spur and into a narrow chimney. Even though I couldn't see him, I knew what he was doing. An hour earlier I had crawled into that same chimney, getting myself stuck. I was wedged in so tight that after a few minutes my right leg had started trembling—a bad case of "sewing machine leg."

But now I felt the rope go slack and knew that Rick had gotten himself free. He was climbing again. A minute later he poked his head over the edge of the cliff. Grinning from ear to ear, he pulled himself on top of the rock.

"All *right!*" he shouted. "This is *great!*"

I couldn't have agreed more. It wasn't the most challenging climb in the world, but to a bunch of seventeen-year-olds it was as exciting as climbing the Matterhorn.

Rick was just unclipping his harness when Al Davis, our high school recreation teacher, trotted up behind us. Al was one of my heroes. During class he had taught us about rock climbing and rappelling. He had let us practice rappelling off the high school bleachers, and he had taken us on a few easy climbs in Rock Canyon. Now—on his day off—he had taken us up Diamond Fork Canyon for a more realistic experience.

That wasn't the only thing Al ever did for me. He taught me how to cross-country ski, and he often let me borrow skis from the high school over the weekend. When I was on my mission to Japan, he wrote to me one Christmas. His letter wasn't long—only a couple of paragraphs—but it put me on cloud nine for weeks. And I still have it.

The nice thing about Al was that he came during a crucial time in my life. Like many teenagers, I was struggling to find myself. I was trying to discover who I was. I worried about my friends, my future, and my self-image.

In the midst of all that, Al made me feel special. He taught me self-reliance, gave me challenges to overcome, and helped me learn about myself. At a time when I felt my life was going nowhere, he gave me a nudge in the right direction and got me moving again.

I know another man named Mel who did the same thing for me. He gave me my first job at Scout camp and changed my life forever. Up until then I was doubting that I would ever serve a mission. But because of Mel, I came away from camp with my enthusiasm sparked and my testimony recharged. I was raring to go!

One of the things I appreciated most about Mel was that he treated me like an adult. Even though I was just eighteen, he trusted me with the same responsibilities as any of the adult staff members. He made me feel important, and he influenced me in ways that he never even knew about.

There will be adults like Al and Mel who will influence your life, too. Maybe you know some of them right now. If not, be assured that you will.

When I was in high school there was an English teacher named Cheryl. I was never in any of her classes, but I can't count the times my friends and I showed up on her doorstep to visit. She was always willing to talk and encourage us and maybe even give us a little advice about the girls we were dating.

She, too, knew how to make me feel special. Because of her interest I was a better, more successful teenager.

Men and women like Al, Mel, and Cheryl made me want to be my best. They can do the same for you. They can put you on a collision course with success.

Seek them out!

The world is full of adults who are willing to sacrifice their time and energy to make you a better person.

They can change your life. They can reach inside and pull out your very best self.

Let them!

In a previous chapter I mentioned a man named Hal. I worked for him at Scout camp, and like Mel, he was never too busy to listen or help if I had a problem. He helped me, encouraged me, pushed me, and drew out of me talents and abilities I didn't even know I had.

Even after camp was over, it wasn't unusual for Hal to call me on the phone once in a while just to see how I was doing. And he never failed to ask, "Is there anything I can do for you?"

Hal was in a stake presidency at the time, which meant that he was a busy, busy man. But he still took time out for me. He helped me to be a better person.

Of all the adults I've ever known, though, none has ever been as important to me as my parents. While I was on my mission I received letters from my mother and father every week. And I was the envy of the mission. Most elders received weekly letters from their mother *or* father, but usually not from both.

But my parents never missed a week. And they wrote wonderful letters. My dad was a detective at the time, and in every letter he included stories about his latest adventures. I loved 'em. And so did my companions.

I remember coming home for dinner with my companion one night to find the two elders who shared our apartment waiting for us.

"You got a letter from your dad," Elder Larsen said. "Hurry and open it!"

On the hardest days, there was nothing like getting a letter from home to cheer me up. And between all the fun "cop" stories, my parents always had words of love and encouragement for me. They kept me going through even the hardest times.

My parents have done a thousand other things for

me. Chances are, your parents have done the same for you.

As you're growing up and have occasional run-ins with adults, it's easy to develop an "us-against-them" attitude toward them. But that's not good. The right adults can shape, mold, and change your life. They can draw a best from you that you never knew you had.

Let them!

Do this: Take a piece of paper and list three adults you admire. They might be men or women with interesting careers or hobbies. Or maybe they're just people who stand out because they're fun.

Now, get to know them! Strike up a conversation if you see them in church, or walk over for a talk if they happen to live nearby. Give them a chance to bless your life.

This might seem scary, but the world is full of adults who enjoy teenagers. And just as they can shape and change your life, you might just be doing the same thing for them. Your youthful energy and zest for life can inspire people many times your age.

I have a young friend named Rob whose grandfather is a retired judge. At family gatherings, the older folks all gather around him to talk and discuss the issues of the day. Rob told me that it's all pretty boring.

"What do they talk about that's so boring?" I asked.

"It's not what they talk about that's boring," he said. "It's just that I'm too young to join in."

That surprised me. I loved talking with Rob. One time I got up at five o'clock on a frosty November morning so I could sit with him on the bank of the Provo River while he filled a requirement for the Environmental Science merit badge. He could talk for hours on sports, mysteries, animals, and just about anything else you wanted to bring up.

People who thought he was too young to join the conversation really missed out.

Remember that as a teenager you have insights and perspectives that might never occur to an older person.

Yes, it's a grown-up's world. But it belongs to you too. So don't believe that in order to be part of it you have to be twenty-one, home from your mission, or married. Attack life now with all the energy you have. Look at adults not as dictators who are there to rule your life but as *partners* who can help shape your life. Learn to work *with* them and not against them.

If you do this, not only will your teenage years begin to flourish but also you'll find yourself on a collision course with success, victory, and happiness. You won't have to wait for success. Chances are, you'll already be there!

Tips to Remember

- Make a list of adults you admire—people who have interests similar to yours or who seem interesting. Then get to know them. Give them a chance to bless your life!

- Never be afraid to associate with an adult. Adults' experiences and abilities can enrich your life. And chances are, they'll enjoy your company too. You'll bless their life as much as they bless yours.

- Don't think that you have to be grown up to be successful in this world. Rear back and charge into life like a gangbuster! Give school, your job, your friends, and your family all the energy and enthusiasm you have.